The Sinopedia Series

China's National
Defense

The Sinopedia Series

CHINA'S NATIONAL DEFENSE

PENG GUANGQIAN
ZHAO ZHIYIN
LUO YONG

CENGAGE Learning™

CHINA INTERCONTINENTAL PRESS

Australia • Brazil • Japan • Korea • Mexico • Singapore • Spain • United Kingdom • United States

China's National Defense
Peng Guangqian, Zhao Zhiyin,
Luo Yong

Publishing Director:
Paul Tan

Editorial Manager:
Yang Liping

Associate Development Editor:
Tanmayee Bhatwadekar

Associate Development Editor:
Joe Ng

Senior Product Director:
Janet Lim

Product Managers:
Kevin Joo
Lee Hong Tan

Assistant Publishing Manager:
Pauline Lim

Production Executive:
Cindy Chai

Translators:
Ma Chenguang
Yan Shuang

Copy Editor:
Mahtab Dubash

Cover Designer:
Ong Lay Keng

Compositor:
Integra Software Services,
Pvt. Ltd.

ISBN-13: 978-981-4319-80-5

ISBN-10: 981-4319-80-5

Cengage Learning Asia Pte Ltd
5 Shenton Way #01-01
UIC Building
Singapore 068808

Cengage Learning is a leading provider of customized learning solutions with office locations around the globe, including Singapore, the United Kingdom, Australia, Mexico, Brazil and Japan. Locate your local office at: **www.cengage.com/global**

Cengage Learning products are represented in Canada by Nelson Education, Ltd.

For product information, visit **www.cengageasia.com**

Printed in Singapore
1 2 3 4 5 12 11 10

Table of Contents

Chapter 1

China's Peaceful Development and National Defense

Every nation must have its own national defense system for a nation can neither exist independently nor can its people enjoy peace without a well-developed defense system in place. National defense came into being with the emergence of states and the need for having a dedicated system that served in the nation's best interest. National defense assures a nation's security, dignity, and social development.

The Charter of the United Nations, which was adopted in 1945, stipulates in Article 1 that the Purpose of the Charter is "to maintain international peace and security," "to take effective collective measures for the prevention and removal of threats to peace, and for the suppression of acts of aggression or other breaches of peace." Building national defense and safeguarding people's peaceful labor are the basic rights and sacred duty bestowed on a sovereign state by international law.

As we moved into the 21st century, the devastating effects of the world wars gradually faded from people's memory. And, although the cause of world peace has steadily advanced, the world is not yet peaceful. Power politics and the root causes of war still exist; strategic expansion, ethnic disputes, religious conflicts, and fighting for domain and resources lead to wars periodically. Given that the global community still lacks effective enforcement mechanisms to prevent the re-emergence of war, strengthening national defense and resisting aggression have become the foundation for the existence and development of a sovereign state.

Profound Learnings from China's History

China is the only nation in the world that has a 5,000-year-old history with an unbroken civilization. In ancient China, which was largely an agrarian society, the Chinese people toiled endlessly on their farmlands.

Contemporary China witnessed repeated foreign aggressions, devastation, and oppression. Since the 1800s, the Western powers, which ascended to prominence during the industrial revolution, were eager to seek world markets and exploit strategic resources. Using the weaponry developed during the industrial revolution, these Western powers launched repeated wars of aggression and plunder against China, including the First Opium War launched by the British colonial army in the 19th century; the Second Opium War, by the joint forces of Britain and France; the First Sino-Japanese War, by the Japanese military in 1895; the aggressive war, by the Eight-Power Allied Forces in the early 1900s; the Russo-Japanese War (1904–1905), which was fought on Chinese soil by the two imperialist countries of Japan and Russia battling for colonization; and the comprehensive war of aggression launched by the Japanese militarists against

Monument to the People's Heroes at Tian'anmen Square, Beijing. Dedicated to millions of Chinese who lost their lives in the fight for national independence and liberation since the Opium War in 1840.

A veteran solider at Marco Polo Bridge, July 7, 2007. Nine soldiers who had participated in the Marco Polo Bridge Incident on July 7, 1937 visited the place 70 years later to mark the moment in history.

China. All these wars caused large-scale devastation in China. The Opium Wars, in particular, can be said to be the biggest, the murkiest, and the most shameless drug wars in world history, while the comprehensive aggression against China by the Japanese militarists was the most barbaric, the most brutal, and the bloodiest war.

On the eve of the First Opium War fought between 1840 and 1842, Western powers smuggled 40,000 chests of opium into China in exchange for 20 million taels of silver from China. The Western colonists carved out spheres of influence on Chinese land through means of war and established modes of extraterritoriality, sought secession of Chinese territory, extorted huge sums of silver taels from China, massacred locals, and exploited Chinese resources. Between the Treaty of Nanking signed between China and Britain on August 29, 1842 and the Sino-US Treaty of Friendship, Commerce, and Navigation signed on November 14, 1948, the Chinese government was forced consecutively by various foreign powers to sign a total of 1,175 treaties, among which 862 were signed with Britain, France, the United States, Japan, Germany, and Russia, accounting for 75% of the total. Most of the treaties were biased and subdued the population into slavery. Through such unequal treaties such as the Treaty of Nanking, the Treaty of Beijing, the Treaty of Tianjin (Tientsin), the Yili Treaty, the Treaty of Shimonoseki, the Protocol of 1901, the Treaty of Lhasa, and the Yantai Treaty, the western powers, in 1901, extorted from China war compensation equaling 1.953 billion yuan in silver coins, equivalent to 16 times the financial income of the government of Qing Dynasty (1644–1911), or 82 times the national

The 70th anniversary ceremony in memory of the 300,000 Chinese compatriots killed by Japanese invaders on December 13, 1937 during the Nanjing Massacre. The ceremony, held in Nanjing of East China's Jiangsu Province, also marked the Nanjing International Day of Peace rally.

total industrial and mineral funding. As for the aggression by the Japanese militarists, their crimes are too numerous to record. The aggressive war against China led to the death or injury of 30 million Chinese servicemen and civilians, of which, as many as 300,000 Chinese citizens were cruelly killed during the Nanking Massacre. The war also caused China a direct economic loss of at least US$100 billion, and an indirect economic loss of more than US$500 billion. This was not only the darkest period in Chinese history alone but also in world history.

Today, China has marched proudly onto the world stage determined to face the future through peaceful cooperation with all. But, history should never be forgotten so that tragedies are never repeated. A nation that forgets the past can never grasp today and create tomorrow. By drawing lessons from bitter experience, the Chinese people have come to realize the vital importance of building a national defense, and have become determined and confident in building a strong and modernized national defense to safeguard national sovereignty and security.

The Fundamental Guarantee of Peace and Development

Peace is China's consistent pursuit, while development is the primary task for China. China's reform and opening up has been an ongoing endeavor for the last 30 years. China's peaceful development is not only changing the face of the nation but also becoming a positive factor in influencing the comprehensive development of the world, including the Asia-Pacific region, in the spheres of politics, economy, military, society, and culture.

History has shown that peaceful development has never been a smooth straight road. Only a consolidated national defense can provide reliable strategic support, ensure peaceful development, and help safeguard a stable external environment needed for progress. Currently, as the world situation continues to undergo profound and complicated changes, China's peaceful development faces unprecedented opportunities and challenges. Strong national defense has always been considered to be of utmost importance and remains one of the major symbols of a nation's strength. Military strength and security still exert a major influence on the evolution of international strategic structure, and strong national defense continues to play an irreplaceable role in safeguarding national security and national interests. At present, though peace and development is the main theme, unstable and uncertain factors threatening peace and development are also on the rise, and traditional and non-traditional factors that posed as threats to security remain intertwined. The comprehensive nature, complexity, and variability of threats to security are exerting an important influence on China's security environment, posing pressures on the safeguarding of national security. China is facing a period of strategic opportunities in building a moderately prosperous society in all respects, which is not only a "golden period of development" where a great deal can be accomplished but also a "period of prominent contradictions" facing many security threats and challenges.

Along with the evolution of an international strategic structure, the transfer of the international competition focus and the strategic objectives of various countries, as well as the acceleration and expansion of the economic globalization process, China's new security issues concerning political security, economic security, cultural security, and information security are becoming prominent. Although China's political and economic structural reforms have led to tremendous development, the perfection of the socialist democratic political system and the establishment of the socialist market economic structure are not likely to be smooth-sailing and cannot be achieved overnight. The complicated situation facing China's peaceful development will determine the difficulty level of the country's task in contemporary national defense building.

China's national defense is the strong pillar and backbone for China's peaceful development, and is also the prerequisite and fundamental safeguard of China's peaceful development. Building a strong national defense is entirely consistent with China's march toward peaceful development.

The Security Environment

Complex Geopolitical Safety Environment

As China is situated on the eastern edge of the Eurasian continent and at the juncture of the geo-strategic interests of big powers, its national security is to a large extent influenced by the strategic competition of big powers, resulting in many variables and complex geo-environmental security.

China is one of the eastern nations on the Eurasian continental chessboard, which is the world's geopolitical center, and is situated at the junction of the Eurasian continental and marine geostrategic area. China connects such strategic regions as Northeast Asia, Southeast Asia, West Asia, and Central Asia. The Asia-Pacific region where China is located is one of the world's most populated regions and an area with the highest concentration of big nations. Seven of the world's top 10 countries, each with a population surpassing 100 million, are situated in this region. This region is a hot spot for important contemporary issues in the world and crisis outbreak points. Among the world's widely acknowledged five major power centers, the United States, China, Russia, and Japan are all concentrated here, with the exception of Europe. The major members of the world's nuclear club, the de facto nuclear states, and countries on the verge of attaining nuclear capability status have formed a concentrated nuclear distribution rim around China, with such a high density of stored nuclear weapons that it can destroy humankind many times over. In particular, varying degrees of interest conflicts exist among the mainstay of various nuclear powers, and if any nuclear crises were to occur, they would undoubtedly have a catastrophic influence on China. As the junction of the Eurasian continental geo-strategic area and the marine geostrategic area, the region has always been a hotly contested spot for various strategic powers in the past.

The Fringe Strategy School considers this region strategic to capture pivotal areas, and the School of Sea Power Strategy views it as a bridgehead in marching onto the land, while the School of Land Power sees the region as a strategic hub sitting proudly on the Eurasian continent and radiating to the sea. Since the mid-1800s, the Western powers had gathered here to engage in fighting in a bid to carve up China. During the Cold War period, this "Oriental

The Administrative Divisions of China.

Outpost" witnessed confrontation between the two major strategic powers, and was an important front undergoing East-West containment and counter-containment, blockade and counter-blockade, siege and anti-siege, which lasted for nearly half a century. After the end of the Cold War, the bipolar structure disintegrated and the international strategic structure became skewed. During the formation of a new strategic structure, all strategic powers launched fierce competition on this soil to vie for an advantageous position in the new structure, and the region where current-day China stands is still in turmoil.

For a long time, China has adhered to the Five Principles of Peaceful Coexistence, and has maintained a good neighborly policy of friendship and partnership. Moreover, China enjoys traditional friendship with the majority of its neighboring countries, and similar histories, and a common desire of safeguarding peace and developing the economy. On the whole, China maintains peaceful and friendly relations of cooperation with its neighboring countries. However, it cannot be denied that China's neighboring countries have different distribution and composition of nationalities, different levels

Negotiators attend the Six-Party Talks in Beijing, on the Korean nuclear issue. China has always advocated peaceful dialogues to solve regional security issues.

of economic development, different religious beliefs and cultural traditions, and major regional and interregional disparities. Coupled with historical and practical reasons, China is prone to various kinds of conflicts and frictions, many of which are remnants of old and new colonial structure as well as hegemony.

The Yongshu Reef in Nansha Islands (dubbed as the gate to China's southern territory).

The evolution of domestic economic, political, and military situations of the neighboring countries, their policies toward China, and the change in relations among the neighboring countries cannot help but exert a significant impact on China's security environment.

This geo-security environment calls for the necessity of building Chinese national defense forces so as to effectively deal with various possible complicated situations.

Development of World Military and Challenges for the New Military Revolution

Since the 1970s, a military revolution characterized by incorporation of information technology (IT) has been developing worldwide. The United States was the first to join this revolution in military affairs based on its strong national power and military strength. It comprehensively promoted the transformation in the military way of thinking, military theory, military structure, and weapons and equipment systems, with the aim of building an IT-based operation platform, and building intelligent, network-based, all-round and all-dimensional armed forces, thus becoming the "leader" in the new contemporary revolution in military affairs. In the Gulf War, the Kosovo War, the War in Afghanistan, and the Iraqi War launched since the 1990s, the United States displayed and demonstrated its military effectiveness obtained from promoting and inculcating IT. A few dozen other countries in the Americas, Europe, and Asia also underwent a military revolution. They mapped development strategies and finalized the development focus based on their own national conditions and military situation. They also

Fishing Patrol No. 311. China's largest fishing administration ship on its tour of inspection to the Xisha Islands in the South China Sea.

increased national defense inputs, elevated the position of military modernization from the standpoint of enhancing national strategic capacities, expedited the building of IT-based operation systems, and comprehensively strengthened national defense and improved the IT level of the armed forces.

With the advent of the 21st century, the new world-wide military revolution increased its pace. This revolution not only helped increasingly change the face and form of modern warfare but also intensified the growing imbalance of military power in the world, leading to the reorganization of the international strategic structure and redrawing of the world's political map. The further development of the worldwide military systems is fundamentally changing the material elements of the balance of the strategic forces of various countries in the world. Industrial and technological advantages are giving way to IT advantages. The full extent of IT-based combat systems and strength of IT-based combat abilities are becoming the key measure of an adoptee country's level of strategic capabilities, and of determining that country's safety factors and its position in future international strategic structure. In this major historical military revolution, the "technological gap" in IT building is increasingly turning into a "strategic gap" of national abilities. As a result, the conscious awareness of this military revolution, the size of input, and the effectiveness of the revolution will probably have a decisive influence on a country's rise and fall as well as its final safety. This will be a significant test for any country's preparedness and innovative ability, and also poses a serious challenge for every nation's future. Seen from the development trend of the contemporary world military, this kind of gap will further widen if no effective measures are taken to strengthen the building of national defense systems and undertaking modernization of the combat abilities on IT-based warfare. If the balance goes out of control, a new round of "epoch difference" will probably appear. The militarily and technologically superior Western powers that used their weaponry against China's machetes and spears once upon a time, is likely to evolve into a military that is technologically far superior against China's mechanization and semi-mechanization, posing a severe threat to China's national security. Given this scenario, China has no other alternative but to strengthen and modernize its national defense systems and thus, circumvent historical mistakes. Strengthening national defense and the armed forces is of vital importance to the long-term development and destiny of China.

The Increasing Prominence of Non-traditional Security

The modern world is witnessing a rise in non-traditional security risks, arising from terrorism, drug trafficking, proliferation of weapons of mass destruction (WMDs), attacks on information networks, ethnic and religious conflicts, transnational crimes, economic refugees and illegal immigrants, economic and financial crises, energy security, and ecological and environmental problems. These have become the global security issues. China is no exception.

Servicemen from the Shandong Provincial Contingent of the Chinese People's Armed People conducting drills with an anti-terrorism assault vehicle in Jinan, Shandong Province, on July 2, 2008, to beef up Olympic security.

Threats to economic security Since China's reform and opening up during the past 30-odd years, the country has maintained fast growth. However, under the backdrop of steady and fast economic growth, potential economic insecurity has continued to persist. First, economic relations between China and the world are becoming more and more complicated, and its sensitivity to the outside world is on the rise.

China's armed forces: the fundamental guarantee for the country's national security.

"THREE FORCES"

Religious extremism, ethnic separatist forces, and violent terrorist forces are the current three forces to be wary of. The "Three Forces" emerged under the disguise of religious extremism and the pretext of "national independence." On one hand, disruptive elements fabricated stories to garner public opinion and confuse people, while on the other hand, these elements carried out violent terrorist activities to sabotage social stability. Their fundamental aim is to create chaos and split the Xinjiang Uygur Autonomous Region from China so as to realize the so-called "independence" of Xinjiang.

Along with the dramatic increase in China's foreign trade volume, the country's trade friction and disputes with other countries in recent years are growing. Second, the influence and pressure of the world economy on China are becoming increasingly prominent. With further opening of its market and investment scope, foreign goods have begun swarming into the country in large numbers, while multinationals are endeavoring to expand businesses in China, which has not only brought competitive pressure to the country's domestic enterprises but also forced China's economic and industrial structures to readjust. Meanwhile, China's economic sovereignty is facing more and more interference from the outside.

Threats to information security The development and wide application of IT has profoundly changed people's lives, accelerating the development and modernization of the country adopting it. However, due to the characteristics of IT itself, and especially the non-border features of information and networks, great information security risks exist in the process of IT modernization. China's information security is currently facing various challenges. Basic information technology is heavily dependent on foreign countries, while the country lacks effective management and technological transformation on introduced technology and equipment in terms of information security. The awareness on information security is weak, while the R&D on information security and the intensity of training given to information security personnel is insufficient.

A number of hostile forces have regularly been launching attacks on China's networks, and carrying out publicity competition, moral infiltration, and cultural aggression, thus threatening the security and stability of the Chinese society.

Risk of terrorism The "9/11 incident" has made nations realize that terrorism has become a major threat to world peace and stability. Terrorist activities in China's neighboring regions are becoming increasingly rampant, and are infiltrating and spreading into Chinese's territory. The "three forces" launched from foreign countries are colluding with each other and with the three evil forces within the Chinese territory. Under the shelter, support, and instigation of international anti-China forces, they are stirring up disorder, creating severe harm to social stability and ethnic harmony as well as public safety along China's border regions. Terrorists and national separatists have become the cause of disasters endangering national security and regional stability.

The Question of Taiwan amid the Core National Interests

Taiwan has always been a sacred part of China's territory. The Question of Taiwan not only involves China's general and particular interests but also relates to its core national interests. It is also the key question concerning China's national security.

Compatriots on both sides of the Taiwan Straits are communities with blood bonds, and China is the common homeland of the compatriots on both sides of the Straits. For the Chinese nation, safeguarding the integrity of national territory and sovereignty as well as ethnic unity is not a short-term political demand and general political choice, but comes from a strong sense of history over thousands of years, a national sentiment deeply rooted in the Chinese civilization from the past 5,000 years, as well as the essence of the traditional cultural heritage of the Chinese nation. Since the Qin Dynasty (221–206 BC) established China's first unified multi-ethnic country creating a new epoch of unification in Chinese history, unification has always occupied a dominant position in China's political life and national sentiment. Unification is regarded as "the regular canon of Heaven and Earth, and the coherent rule of past and present." It is regarded as the spiritual bond between all members of the Chinese nation, and is a powerful driving force and an important guarantor of a multi-ethnic country enduring repeated disasters. Although there were situations in which several short-lived powers co-existed in Chinese history, unification has always been the mainstay in the development of Chinese history. After each short-lived rule of separated powers, the country would return to reunification. The time under a reunified China has been the longest thus far, while the scale of the reunification is becoming larger and the voice of the reunification stronger. It can be even said that the longer the time of rule

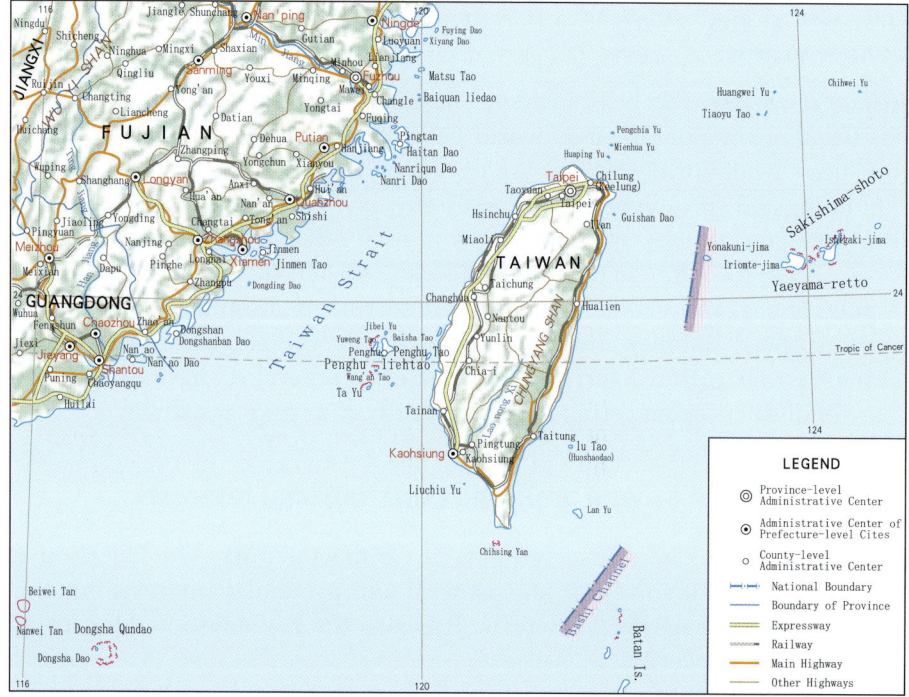

Map of Taiwan Straits.

by separated powers, the stronger the desire of the people seeking reunification and the greater the voice of the people calling for reunification.

Under the short-lived rules by separate powers, the parties concerned did not believe that separation of powers was a normal state. What they pursued was not a long-term and fixed situation of rule by separate powers, but the opportunity to grab the legitimate position and become the dominant power in establishing reunification. Dr. Sun Yat-sen (1866–1925), the great forerunner of the Chinese democratic revolution, noted that "unification is the hope of the whole Chinese nation, the wish of the people, and Heaven and the Earth should follow it." This polymerization idea of "unification" in Chinese culture is quite different from the "fission" way of "divide and rule" in the West. It condenses the deep feeling that, throughout the centuries, the Chinese nation believed that blood is thicker than water. It carries the ideal of sharing a common destiny in life or death, and of experiencing fortune and misfortune together. It is the highest value of the Chinese nation, which should never be tarnished.

As the maritime outpost and coastal barrier in China's southeastern coastal waters, Taiwan is a vital ocean communications hub in the western Pacific and, together with the Chinese mainland, has always been involved in mutual protection and formed an integrated body in offensive and defensive safeguards. Taiwan cannot be separated from the Chinese mainland. Without the backing of the mainland's vast territory stretching as much as 9.6 million square kilometers, Taiwan will be an isolated island. It can easily fall prey to stronger elements and annexation by foreign powers and witness the repeated tragedy of becoming a colony as in the past. At the same time, the Chinese mainland cannot lose Taiwan either. If Taiwan fell into the hands of foreign enemies and separatist forces, the island will lose its role as a barrier, leaving open the door to the Chinese mainland, and the country's whole strategic defense at sea will be suddenly lost, and its defense system compromised. Moreover, Taiwan will by then further become the springboard and stronghold of foreign enemies in attacking the Chinese mainland, serving as an "unsinkable aircraft carrier" endangering the safety of the Chinese mainland. Obviously, the Chinese people have no room for compromise when it concerns national security.

Chapter 2

A New Concept of Security and the Defensive National Defense Policy

The Great Wall in northern China was the most magnificent and largest strategic defense project in ancient China. It is the materialization and epitome of strategic defensive thought of the Chinese nation, as well as the symbol of China's defensive national defense policy. China's defensive national defense policy is deeply rooted in the country's outstanding strategic cultural heritage, while the ideological foundation of China's defensive national defense policy is the new concept of security China has always advocated.

New Concept of Security: Mutual Trust, Mutual Benefit, Equality, and Coordination

The so-called New Concept of Security refers to the most common views and concepts on security issues. The country's concept of security includes the fundamental recognition and fundamental concept of basic security issues surrounding the identification of security interests and the nature of security, judgment of security environment and security relations, pursuit of security objectives and security order, as well as security channels and security methods. It plays an internal decisive role in planning and formulating the country's security strategy and security policies.

In the mid-20th century, the East and the West once staged a long-term confrontation following the end of World War II, and the concept of security was mainly expressed in confrontation security, group security, unilateral security, and absolute safety. This concept of security was characterized by a Cold War mentality and "zero-sum" thinking, stressing that everything should be divided in accordance with the similarities and differences of ideological and social systems, while enemies and friends are also differentiated in accordance with the similarities and differences of ideological forms and social systems. It also emphasized that security is a confrontational "zero-sum" relation featured by the simple choice between loss and gain—gain on one side through the sacrifice of the other—believing that the security of the opposite side is the insecurity of one's own, while the power of other players is a challenge to one's own security, and in particular, the power of a country which has a different political system forms the greatest challenge. As a result, this kind of security mentality did not bring peace and security, but finally created an increasingly serious war crisis. In order to establish security, the two sides of the Cold War confrontation built a military weapon with the capacity to destroy humankind many times over. However, instead of bringing security to any one side, it further intensified the sense of insecurity.

Following the end of the Cold War, great changes have taken place in the international strategic structure and security environment. Since the advent of the 21st century, human society has entered a new period of historic transformation. The accelerated advancement in technology such as the introduction of IT into technology patterns, global economic integration, the multi-polarization of strategic patterns, democratization of international relations as well as high-tech orientation of the military, has rapidly changed the outlook of human society and the structure of international security. Unprecedented global economic integration has helped deepen the interdependence between the interests of various countries, while international cooperation in production, cross-border flow of capital, and global commodity exchange have all promoted integration of various nations, creating a meshwork of all involved parties being bound together. Human society has never been more closely linked, and faces increasingly common security issues and safety concerns. The potential devastation that modern warfare can cause has increasingly stemmed the onset of war, creating a paradoxical situation between the need for war and its means.

Under the new security environment, it is difficult for a country to maintain its security by waging a war. Similarly, it is difficult to maintain security on the basis of another country's insecurity. It is the objective requirement and the call of the times for the world to seek peace, for people everywhere to work with mutual cooperation, for countries to seek development, and for societies to seek progress. After experiencing the catastrophic effects of two world wars and the suffering during the Cold War for half a century, people in all countries long for lasting peace in the world, and look forward to establishing a reasonable security structure and order, and aspire to promote common development and common prosperity, and jointly create a beautiful future for humankind.

Scholars from the strategic defense research institutes of China and the member countries of the Association of Southeast Asian Nations (ASEAN) attend the China-ASEAN senior defense scholars dialogue in Beijing. The dialogue opened on March 12, 2008, and was sponsored by the Academy of Military Science of the Chinese People's Liberation Army.

It is under this backdrop that China has put forward the New Concept of Security aimed at creating a stable, secure, and reliable international peaceful environment, with its core being mutual trust, mutual benefit, equality, and coordination. Under the new historic conditions, by giving full play to and developing the basic spirit of the Five Principles of Peaceful Coexistence, and completely discarding the "Cold War mentality," the New Concept of Security suits the demands of the time and carries universal significance, as well as being another major contribution of China to international relations, in addition to the Five Principles of Peaceful Coexistence. It is fundamentally different from the previous concept on security. The New Concept of Security is aimed at safeguarding peaceful and commonly shared security. Its core ideals of mutual trust, mutual benefit, equality, and coordination are an integrated whole. Mutual trust is the foundation of the New Concept of Security; mutual benefit, its purpose; and coordination, the way to its realization.

Mutual trust is the ideological foundation in safeguarding peace. Mutual trust implies that no country should be suspicious of or hostile to another and that no country should under any pretext regard other countries as enemies or deliberately create an enemy in order to artificially meet the needs of some forces. Because of the multi-polarization of the world, any changes in the balance of power will not pose any threat to world security by itself. What really poses a threat is the relentless pursuit by changing powers of hegemony and power politics. One needs to discard the bias in ideological formation and the Cold War mentality to pursue mutual trust.

Mutual benefit is the material basis in safeguarding peace. The world is becoming an increasingly interrelated and interdependent place. There is realization that the security of a country or a region is dependent on the overall security of the world. With regard to mutual benefit, a country should fully consider and respect the security interests of other countries while realizing its own security interests. In this manner, nations can realize common benefits and security interests, instead of neglecting and harming the legitimate security interest of other countries, thereby avoiding establishing their own security based on the insecurity of others. If a country arbitrarily shifts its own troubles onto others, harms others to benefit itself, and only considers its unilateral security, it is impossible to see genuine security.

Equality is the political basis in safeguarding peace. China maintains that all countries—big or small, rich or poor, strong or weak—are equal members of the international community, have equal right in sharing peace and tranquility and safeguarding their own security interest, and have an equal say in international security affairs. World security affairs should be jointly handled by all countries, instead of letting some pursue special rights unlimited by the international community according to the size of their strength, or engaging in a practice where the big bullies the small, the strong dominates the weak, and the rich oppresses the poor. Every country should respect diversity, oppose any country that controls another country, and oppose the practice in which a certain country or several countries manipulate international security affairs.

Coordination is the way to realize the safeguarding of peace. China maintains that the security issues faced by the world call for every country to cooperate hand in hand. Instead of alliance, exclusivity, creating conflict, or targeting a third country, coordination is an open and new type of security mechanism that is established on the basis of mutual trust, mutual benefit, and equality, and with a purpose of jointly safeguarding peace. It is aimed at eliminating hidden insecure risks and preventing military conflict through dialogues, exploring effective ways in resolving security issues through equal coordination, and overcoming risk through concerted activities instead of resorting to the use and threat of force.

The New Concept of Security that China advocates has discarded the Cold War mentality that identifies and handles national security issues by differentiating foes and friends in accordance with the division in ideological formations and following confrontational "zero-sum" relations. The New Concept of Security has reflected the voice of the times for world peace and development in the new century, showed the general trend of historical development and is in line with the development requirement of the times and the common security interest of the whole world. It has distinct characteristics of the current times, and is a completely new take on security. It is the inheritance and development of the Five Principles of Peaceful Coexistence in the new epoch, a new embodiment of China's outstanding cultural heritage in "regarding harmony as fundamental," and a major theoretical contribution of China to contemporary international politics and international security amid the long strides of its advancement on its road to modernization.

Main Content of China's National Defense Policy

Based on the New Concept of Security, China pursues a defensive national defense policy. The fundamental task of China's national defense is to safeguard national security and territorial integrity and sovereignty, and safeguard

CHINA'S NATIONAL DEFENSE POLICY

- Safeguarding national security and protecting the interest of national development
- Achieving comprehensive, coordinated, and sustainable development of national defense and army building in keeping with coordinated development of the economy and national defense
- Strengthening the quality of the army through informatization.
- Implementing the military strategy of active defense
- Adhering to a nuclear policy of self-defense, implementing the nation's nuclear policy and nuclear strategy, and deterring hostile forces from using or threatening to use nuclear weapons against China
- Positively fostering a security environment conducive to China's peaceful development

the realization of the strategic objectives in building a moderately prosperous society in all respects. Strengthening national defense and the armed forces occupies an important place in the overall plan for the cause of socialism with Chinese characteristics. The key points of China's national defense policy are as follows:

- **Safeguarding national security and protecting the interest of national development.**
  We must prevent and deflect invasions, and ensure that the country's territorial waters, airspace, and borders are not violated. We must oppose and curb the splitting activities of "Taiwan independence," prevent and fight all forms of terrorism, separatism, and extremism. The armed forces must fully carry out its historical missions, enhance the military's capability to respond to various security threats and accomplish diverse military tasks, and ensure that the military is able to effectively deal with crises, safeguard peace, curb wars, and win wars in various complicated situations.

- **Achieving comprehensive, coordinated, and sustainable development of national defense and army building in keeping with the development of the economy and national defense.**
  We must incorporate strengthening of national defense and the armed forces into the overall strategy of the country's modernization drive, allow the national defense and army modernization process to be in sync with the country's modernization process, and pay attention to the compatible development between a defense-oriented economy and a socio-economy, between military technology and civilian technology, and between military professionals and civilian professionals such that national defense and economic development promote each other and realize the unity of making our country prosperous and our armed forces powerful, in the process of building a moderately prosperous society in all respects.

- **Strengthening the quality of the army through informatization. Building a lean and strong military force in the Chinese way and exercising the combination of a streamlined standing army with a powerful reserve force for national defense.**
  The military should step up its efforts to build a joint operational command system, training system, and support system for fighting wars in the information age, enhance the building of systems integration of services and arms, optimize the structure of forces, especially the internal structure of the services and arms, and improve the organization of troops.

  The People's Liberation Army (PLA) pursues a strategy of strengthening itself by means of science and technology, and works to accelerate changes in war-fighting capabilities by drawing on scientific and technological advances. The PLA seeks to raise its capabilities of independent innovation in weaponry and equipment, establish and improve systems of weapons and equipment research and manufacturing, achieve military personnel training and logistics that integrate military with civilian purposes and combine military efforts with civilian support, build the armed forces through diligence and thrift, and blaze a path of development with Chinese characteristics featuring military and civilian integration. The military should gradually establish a modern national defense mobilization system that is centralized and unified, well-structured, swiftly responsive, authoritative, and efficient. The PLA should actively explore new channels and new methods characterized by the integration of military economy and civilian economy, and bring together soldiers and civilians to face new situations, so as to allow for the building of national defense and the armed forces to better combine with economic and social development in wider scope, at higher and deeper levels, and fully promote military-civilian combination in all spheres of the economy, science and technology, education, and personnel. The military should enhance the scientific and technological content of training; make innovations in the content, forms, and methods of training; actively promote the strategic project of personnel construction; and cultivate a large group of new types of military personnel to master modern warfare.

- **Implementing the military strategy of active defense.**
  The PLA should ensure that it is well prepared to win local wars under the information age, upgrade and develop the strategic concept of the people's war, work for close coordination between the military and political, economic, diplomatic, cultural, and legal endeavors, use strategies and tactics in a comprehensive way, and take the initiative to prevent and defuse crises and deter conflicts and wars. Considering joint operations as the basic strategy, the PLA aims to bring the operational strengths of different services and arms into full play and raise its defense capabilities and combat effectiveness under high-tech conditions.
- **Adhering to a nuclear policy of self-defense, implementing the nation's nuclear policy and strategy, and deterring hostile forces from using or threatening to use nuclear weapons against China.**
  China remains firmly committed to the policy of "no first use" of nuclear weapons at any time and under any circumstances. It unconditionally undertakes not to use or threaten to use nuclear weapons against non-nuclear-weapon states or nuclear-weapon-free zones, and stands for the comprehensive prohibition and complete elimination of nuclear weapons. China upholds the principles of counterattack in self-defense and limited development of nuclear weapons, and aims at building a lean and effective

nuclear force capable of meeting national security needs. It endeavors to ensure the security and reliability of its nuclear weapons and maintains a credible nuclear deterrent force. China's nuclear force is under the direct command of the Central Military Commission. China exercises great restraint in developing its nuclear force. It has never entered and will never enter into a nuclear arms race with any other country.

- **Positively fostering a security environment conducive to China's peaceful development.**

China maintains military contacts with other countries on the basis of the Five Principles of Peaceful Coexistence, and develops cooperative military relations that are non-aligned, non-confrontational, and not directed against any third party. China takes part in international security cooperation, strengthens strategic coordination and consultation with major powers and neighboring countries, and conducts bilateral or multilateral military exchanges. It promotes the establishment of just and effective collective security mechanisms and military confidence-building mechanisms, and works with other countries to prevent conflicts and wars. China stands for effective disarmament and arms control that are just, reasonable, comprehensive, and balanced in nature. China opposes nuclear proliferation and endeavors to advance the process of

Ground-to-air missile force: the sharp knife of national air defense.

international nuclear disarmament. China observes the purposes and principles of the UN Charter, carefully honors its international obligations, and participates in UN peacekeeping operations, international counter-terrorism cooperation, and international disaster relief operations. It plays an active part in maintaining global and regional peace and stability.

Basic Characteristics of China's National Defense Policy

The following are the characteristics of China's national defence policy:

Self-initiative nature
China has always adhered to building and consolidating national defense independently with its own initiatives and through self-reliance. By relying on its own strength to maintain national security, China aims to make its own strategic judgment in accordance with facts, make decisions on national defense, and formulate national defense development strategies independently and with its own initiatives. The country will neither attach itself to anyone and act at the mercy of others nor will it forge alliance with any other country or group, or participate in any military groups.

Self-defensive nature
China's national defense does not pose threats to anyone or infringe upon others. The country firmly opposes hegemony and power politics and is opposed to all types of war, aggression, and expansion policies. China will neither engage in military expansion nor will it launch military bases or military spheres of influence in foreign countries. China does not seek hegemony and will never seek hegemony even if it is developed and becomes stronger. China's modernization drive on national defense is solely for the purpose of self-defense and safeguarding a peaceful environment conducive to nation building. China makes great efforts to prevent and put an end to wars and tries hard to resolve international disputes and problems left over by history through peaceful means.

Defensive nature
China will not take the initiative to attack anyone. The Constitution of the People's Republic of China (PRC) and the National Defense Law of the PRC, which is enacted in accordance with the Constitution, specify the tasks of the armed forces of the PRC as being "to consolidate national defense, resist

aggression, defend the motherland, and safeguard people's peaceful work." The 21st century will be utilized by China to build a moderately prosperous society in all respects and to achieve the great rejuvenation of the Chinese nation. China in the 21st century should safeguard the long-term strategic stability of the country, create strategic postures conducive to the country's sustainable development and provide reliable security safeguards for the realization of modernization and national rejuvenation.

The self-initiative, self-defense, and defensive characteristics of China's contemporary national defense are not carried out with unfettered, subjective discretion. Instead, they are fundamental characteristics determined by China's strategic cultural heritage, the political bases of China's contemporary society, and China's unique development path.

The Continuation of China's Strategic Cultural Tradition

The strategic thought of any country is fundamentally based in its strategic cultural heritage. This is because its strategic cultural tradition was not formed overnight, and will not simply disappear or be subject to variation. So long as a strategic cultural tradition exists, it will take root in the nation's long-term strategic thinking.

The Chinese nation, with 5,000 years of civilization, is one of the world's great peace-loving nations. Historically, Chinese civilization has been based on agriculture as its mainstay. Agricultural civilization helped cultivate the strategic cultural tradition of the Chinese nation featuring ideas such as "loving one's profession while earth bound," and "harmony is the most precious thing."

During its 5,000 years of civilization, although China witnessed a great number of wars, there was hardly any case for it to seek military expansion overseas. The core of China's strategic culture is to pursue ethnic harmony and national unity. China's ancient history of war is mainly a history of unification wars among the Chinese nation and a history of anti-invasion wars in resisting foreign aggression. The attitude toward war by military strategists in the past dynasties in ancient China was to be "cautious of wars" instead of "loving wars." The focus of China's national defense thought, even today, is on defending one-self rather than launching attacks. Our predecessors in the past dynasties have always advocated the ideas that "the world should aim for universal love," that "one should consider harmony as the most precious thing, and put special emphasis on harmony and on people," and "one should not vie for the world through warfare." They believe that "a nation, though strong, will die if it indulges in wars," and "arms are lethal weapons while wars run counter to morals" and "they should only be used when they are absolutely necessary." They pursue an idea of "breaking the enemy's resistance without fighting" and "convincing people with prestige and morality, and subduing the enemy with wisdom."

During the Han Dynasty (206 BC–220 BC) and the Tang Dynasty (618 AD–907 AD), China was the strongest country in the world. However, it did not expand into the space of neighboring nationalities, let alone pose any threat to the outside world. Instead, China kept good neighborly relations with the neighboring ethnic groups and countries through a "policy of mollification," and made its due contribution to the development of human culture, science, and technology with its highly advanced civilization. During the Ming Dynasty (1368–1644), the Chinese mariner, explorer, and diplomat Zheng He led fleets to the "Western Ocean," or oceans between Kalimantan and Africa, in seven voyages from 1405 to 1433 and visited 30-odd countries. His voyage was made half a century earlier than those by Columbus and Vasco da Gama in the West, and the size of his fleet was several times larger than theirs. However, what Zheng He brought to the countries he reached was Chinese porcelain and silk, and the Chinese never tried to establish colonies overseas with their powerful marine forces. This was in sharp contrast to the practices of Western colonists. In contemporary times, China first advocated the Five Principles of Peaceful Coexistence, and has always pursued an independent foreign policy of peace, stressing that the goal of national defense building is solely for self-defense, defending national sovereignty and territorial integrity, and safeguarding people's peaceful work. This is in line with the basic connotation of Confucian thought that "the benevolent loves others" and the strategic cultural tradition emphasizing "harmony is the most precious thing." Since 1949, when New China was founded, the country has witnessed eight strategic military operations, which were all self-defense in nature.

Internal Requirement of China's Current Politics

The founding of New China in 1949 not only brought an end to the country's history of being trampled upon but also rid the country of a political scene of external expansions. The Chinese people, who have greatly suffered aggression at the hands of foreign powers and have gained independence after a long-term struggle and bloody sacrifice, are well aware that national independence and sovereignty have not come easily; they fully realize the preciousness of peace and prosperity. While cherishing their peace and independence won after a long-term struggle, the Chinese people empathize with the wishes and legitimate rights of other countries in safeguarding independence and peace. The sovereignty of New China comes from the people and belongs to the people, and therefore, it must and has to solely serve the interest of the people. It is the sole task and sole purpose of the people's power of New China to forcefully safeguard and lead the Chinese people to engage in peaceful work wholeheartedly, develop productive forces to maximum effect, strengthen comprehensive national strength, improve people's livelihood, and promote people's well-being. Apart from this, there is no other task or purpose.

In line with this purpose, China has formulated a development strategy for developing the national economy and speeding up the modernization drive and has embarked on a path of reform and opening up since the 1970s after ruling out all kinds of interference. The successful implementation of this strategy is gradually changing the country's image in the last century— that of being poor and weak—and will ultimately help the Chinese nation rise and establish its position at the forefront of world civilization once again. This will be a long-term task with historical significance. Realizing this task requires the relentless efforts of several generations and a long-term peaceful and stable internal and external environment. It is necessary that the country groups its financial, personnel, material, and other resources to focus on economic construction to the greatest extent; further, all walks of life, including national defense and military building, are required to serve the general aim of national economic construction. China's national development strategy

Developing undersea oil resources depends on the consolidation of national defense at sea.

has determined that China cannot develop its military forces in an unlimited fashion by departing from the overall situation of the country, and it is even more impossible for the country to discard economic construction, and spend precious national resources on meaningless external expansion and aggression wars. If the country's limited resources are consumed by aggression and expansion, people's welfare will be neglected and the country's prosperity and progress will also be similarly checked. Even if its national economy soars and its people become prosperous, China will continue to unswervingly adhere to this path, and build a socialist and spiritual civilization, so as to further develop socially productive forces, fully meet the growing material and cultural needs of the people, and strive to make a greater contribution to humankind.

Chapter 3

National Defense and Building of Armed Forces based on the Scientific Outlook on Development

The Scientific Outlook on Development is a major strategic thought guiding China in building a moderately prosperous society in all respects in the new century and at the new stage of development. It takes development as its essence, putting people first as its core; comprehensive, balanced, and sustainable development as its basic requirement; and overall consideration as its fundamental approach. The development of national defense and building of the armed forces under the guidance of the Scientific Outlook on Development should be a development carried out within the overall strategic situation of the country's modernization, and adapted to the interest of national security and development. It should be a development giving ample attention to overall construction and the unity of revolutionary, modernized, and standardized construction. It should be development through a people-centered principle, and should promote the coordinated building of the armed forces and the all-round development of officers and soldiers. It should be a development that adheres to the building of a lean and strong military force with Chinese characteristics and the coordination of speed, quality, and efficiency.

Making the Country Prosperous and the Armed Forces Powerful

Making the country prosperous and the armed forces powerful are two indispensable wings of a country's development. Without prosperity, there is no way for a country to make the armed forces powerful, and likewise, without a powerful military force, there is no way to defend the country. In order to stand independently in the world, a nation needs both economic strength and a strong national defense force. The modernization of national defense is unthinkable without economic strength, while the security environment of economic construction cannot be safeguarded without a strong national defense force. In the mid-1800s, contrary to expectations, China's gross national product on the eve of the Opium War was among the highest worldwide. However, due to lack of a strong national defense, coupled with other elements such as political corruption, the country failed to block the invasion of Western powers. Social wealth was reduced to becoming war trophies of the Western powers. In contemporary times, with the rapid development in science and technology, industrial revolution and new revolution in military affairs, the link between national defense building and economic construction is becoming tighter, and the inter-dependency of development of the armed forces and economic and social development is becoming stronger. As a result, it is imperative to consider the relation between economic construction and national defense building at the

China has strengthened the combination of military personnel cultivation and national education.

height of national security. It is equally important to focus on the overall development strategy under the guidance of the Scientific Outlook on Development, and achieve unity in making the country prosperous and the armed forces powerful.

The key is to coordinate national defense building and economic construction and achieve military-civilian integration with Chinese characteristics. China must pay ample attention to integration between the plan of strengthening the national defense and armed forces building and the overall plan of national economic and social development, between science and technology and weaponry development and the development of national science and technology industries, between national defense facilities and battlefield construction and national basic infrastructure construction, between military personnel training and national education, and between the socialization of military logistics and national social service and security system. This is to realize the coordinated development of national defense building and economic construction in scope, scale, and level.

Defense Expenditure to Satisfy Minimum Security Requirements

The defensive nature of China's national defense has determined that the country's defense expenditure will always be limited. It should only be limited in meeting the minimum security requirement on defending national sovereignty and territorial integrity. It is impossible and unnecessary for China to either invest the country's limited resources into an unlimited arms race or to sacrifice people's livelihood to expand its armament arsenal.

Although China's defense spending has witnessed a slight increase in recent years, the allocation of defense spending should always follow the line of coordinated development of national defense building and economic and social development, and should always be subject to the defensive nature of China's national defense policy.

On the basis of steady, stable, and rapid development of the economy and the rapid growth in financial revenue in recent years, the Chinese Government raised the country's defense expenditure moderately. However, the rise is always limited and low, both in absolute as well as relative terms. The rise in China's defense spending in recent years has been far lower than the financial revenue growth. China's defense spending grew by 15.8% annually between 2003 and 2007, far lower than the annual growth rate of 22.1% of financial revenue during the same period.

The plateau with a costly supply line adds to the cost of the national defense.

As compared with other countries, especially some large countries, China's defense spending as a proportion of GDP and financial budget has always stayed at a rather low level. Let's take the year 2007 as an example. The United States' defense spending made up 4.6% of its GDP and 16.6% of its financial budget. For Britain, the rates were 3% and 6.9%; France, 2% and 13.5%; Russia, 2.63% and 15.1%; and India, 2.5% and 14.1%, respectively. However, China's defense spending as a proportion of GDP was only 1.4%, while its defense spending made up 7.2% of its financial budget.

In 2009, China's defense budget hit 480.686 billion yuan, representing an increase of 14.9% over the figure in 2008. However, the military budget and war funding of the United States in fiscal year 2009 reached as much as US$611 billion. Different from the US practice of using the money directly on external wars and expansion of its military superiority, the rise in China's defense expenditure belongs to a compensatory growth in making up for the weak foundation for national defense, and is the normal requirement for safeguarding national security. The increase in China's defense budget in 2009 is mainly used to improve the living conditions of officers and soldiers. In accordance with the level of China's economic and social development and with the growth in income of civil servants and rise of living standards of urban and rural residents, it is imperative to adjust the allowance and subsidy standard for the military accordingly, so as to ensure the corresponding improvement in the standard of living of the military staff. Moreover, the Chinese government not

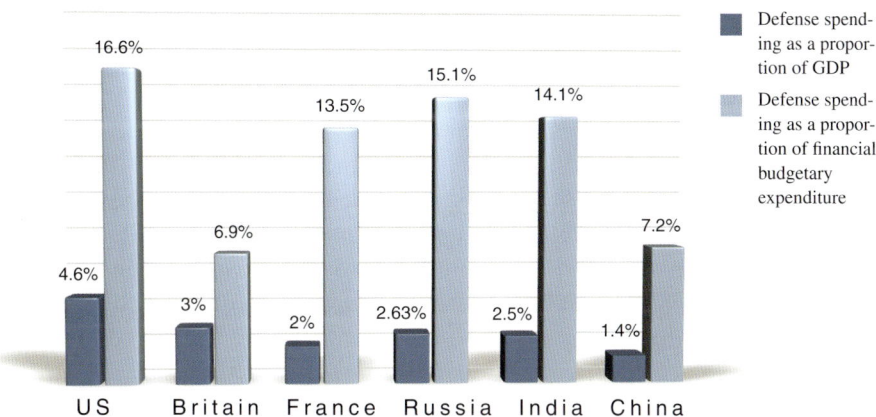

The defense spending of major countries as a proportion of their respective GDP and financial budgetary expenditure

only needs to increase investment in the informatization of the armed forces to meet the needs of revolution in military affairs but also needs to appropriately increase the funds for equipment and its supporting facilities development. In addition, the military must also enhance its emergency response capacity building in non-warfare military operations such as strengthening the disaster relief work of the armed forces, counter-terrorism, and safeguarding stability, improving its capabilities in responding to a variety of security threats and accomplishing diversified military tasks, and supporting the reconstruction of infrastructure for troops affected by the Wenchuan Earthquake in Sichuan Province on May 12, 2008.

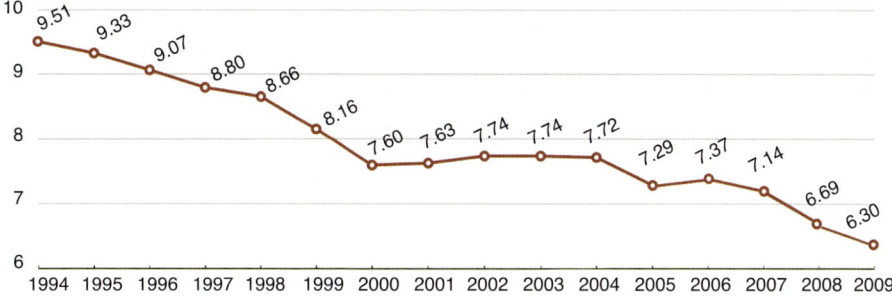

The percentages (%) of defense expenditure in the financial expenditure of China between 1994 and 2009

Since the 1980s, as China concentrated its financial and material resources on economy building, the country's defense input dropped significantly and there were too many outstanding issues to resolve in national defense building, affecting the normal national defense building work. In particular, China's defense spending dropped by 5.83% each year during 1979 and 1989, but during the same period, corresponding prices rose remarkably, especially weaponry prices that doubled, leading to a marked reduction in the actual purchasing power of defense expenditure. As there was no new input, the building of national defense and the armed forces almost came to a halt, and even regressed. Many weapons and equipment, though backward and aging after many years of use, could not be updated even after surpassing their service life. Based on this, China's moderate increase in defense spending is in fact a remedial measure taken to stop the trend of deterioration in defensive capabilities due to the reduced input in the earlier period, and an objective requirement in safeguarding the minimum defense capabilities.

In recent years, a large share of the increased defense expenditure has been raised as maintenance expenses, which are aimed at ensuring that the living standards of military personnel are not lower than the average social level. During the past 15 years, China has raised the board expenses of soldiers

From August 1, 2007, all Chinese People's Liberation Army troops began to adopt the 07' style military uniforms.

and increased the salaries of officers and allowances for soldiers by six times. Meanwhile, in line with social and economic structural reform, it is establishing and gradually improving a social security system for servicemen, such as injury and death insurance for servicemen, medical insurance for demobilized servicemen, and housing subsidies for servicemen.

The appropriate increase in defense expenditure in recent years also reflects the urgent need for safeguarding national sovereignty and territorial integrity and supporting the peaceful development of the country, and to a certain degree, reflects the severe challenge in dealing with the worldwide revolution in military affairs and the need to strive for the modernization of our army. Entering into the 21st century, the world's new revolution in military affairs has been showing a trend of accelerated development. The armed forces in developed countries are realizing a comprehensive transformation from mechanization and IT application, but for China, which is still in the mechanization and semi-mechanization stage, the task of mechanization has not been achieved amid the challenge of informatization. In order to seize opportunities and accomplish the tasks of both mechanization and IT application, China is actively promoting a revolution in military affairs with Chinese characteristics and endeavoring to realize two fundamental transformations. These are that the military struggle preparations should be transformed from being those to win local wars under conditions of informatization to being those based on winning IT-based warfare. At the same time, the building of the armed forces will be transformed from a numerically superior to a qualitatively superior type, and from a manpower-intensive to a technology-intensive type. As a result, the requirement structure of defense expenditure will develop into one that emphasizes technological upgrading, quality enhancement, and structure rationalization, with the requirement of technical services and arms such as the Navy, the Air Force, and the Second Artillery Force steadily upgraded. Thus, there is tremendous pressure to increase China's defense expenditure. The appropriate increase in defense expenditure in recent years is also due in part to the strengthening of technology and technological innovation and the minimum input to avoid widening the new "period gap" with the armed forces in advanced countries.

Giving Full Consideration to All Types of National Defense and Armed Forces Building

To implement the Scientific Outlook on Development, all types of national defense and armed forces building will be encouraged, especially the coordination between mechanization and informatization, combat force building of services and arms, and current and long-term development, so as to promote the healthy and rapid development of defense and the armed forces.

Giving Full Consideration to Mechanization and Informatization Building

With the advancements in science and technology, and the world's new revolution in military affairs, forms of warfare are being transformed from mechanized warfare to IT-based warfare. Informatization has become the prime focus of armed forces building efforts, as those armed forces without informatization capabilities will be eliminated through future wars. Advanced countries have all sped up their construction in informatization, aiming to seek strategic initiative and competitive advantages. The armed forces in China are still in the developmental stage of mechanization and semi-mechanization, and are facing the dual tasks of ramping up mechanization and informatization. In order to accomplish these tasks, it is imperative to accurately grasp the development trend and essence of the world's new revolution in military affairs, and give full consideration to the building of mechanization as well as informatization.

First, let us look at the country's national conditions and military situations. China's economic development as well as scientific and technological progress have provided the conditions and basis for its military development. However, China's economic strength, and scientific and technological levels are not very powerful and advanced. As a result, in accomplishing the tasks of mechanization and informatization building, it is impossible to build informatization as the Western advanced countries have, and the military must leave some things undone while engaging in important matters. China will adhere to the development path in modernization and informatization which aims to gain more benefits with less input.

While considering the building of an IT-based military force and winning IT-based warfare as the strategic objectives, the military should put mechanization as the basis while taking informatization as the lead so as to promote the integrated development of mechanization and informatization and enhance the military's defensive capabilities under the conditions of informatization.

Second, informatization needs to be expedited on the basis of mechanization. Mechanization is the basis of marked progress in informatization, as without mechanization, informatization will be like water without a source and a tree without roots. Informatization is the amplifier of the military's combat power, and is an important milestone in measuring the modernization level of the military in contemporary times.

While promoting mechanization and laying a solid foundation for informatization, China adheres to vigorously promoting informatization of the military. The military should conduct research and development on new and high-tech capabilities centered on IT, strengthen construction on reconnaissance and intelligence, command and control, electronic warfare, and communications systems, and develop equipment for electronic warfare and network warfare, so as to steadily elevate the military's capabilities in IT-based warfare. It is imperative for the military to conduct integration and optimization on system and mechanism such that they have concentrated leadership, unified planning, scientific management, and resource sharing in the spheres of informatization of weaponry, space information system, and integrated electronic information system. The country should strengthen comprehensive integration, and realize the inter-linkage and inter-communication among the intelligence information system, command and control system, and weapons operation platform.

Third, the level of mechanization based on informatization needs to be elevated. Mechanization construction is the basis for informatization building, and the speed and quality of mechanization construction directly influences the process and level of informatization building. The mechanization construction should take informatization as the driving force and strive to improve information content, as mechanization without informatization is mechanization without any future prospects and without any value. At present, the basis of mechanization of China's armed forces is rather weak, and as a result, China has continued to utilize the breakthroughs in mechanization construction during the past few decades to further speed up mechanization. The armed forces should use the informatization requirement to push for the development of mechanization and use informatization to choose, renovate, and reorganize mechanization so as to promote mechanization construction for a high stratum and high level of progress. The military should readjust and innovate its mechanisms and control measures for its structural systems and establishments, personnel cultivation, and military training formulated under the conditions of mechanization in order to adapt to the objective requirements of IT-based warfare.

Fourth, mechanization and informatization should be integrated by focusing on informatization. The armed forces should make mechanization the basis while bringing about informatization, and should follow the path to integrated development of mechanization and informatization. China should then adhere to further mechanization and IT-based weapons and equipment development, development of fire and information power, with an emphasis on information power and integrating mechanization and informatization. The military should pay specific attention to strengthening the building of IT-based weapons and equipment, IT-based combat command system, and IT-based integrated logistics in order to realize the integration of the various systems of intelligence; to command, combat and safeguard, and formulate the IT-based operational system; and to enhance the combat effectiveness of the armed forces under IT-based conditions. The focus should be on optimizing structures, smoothing out relations, enhancing system construction, and elevating the overall combat effectiveness of the armed forces.

Giving Full Consideration to the Combat Force Building of Services and Arms

China's combat forces are reasonably well structured and are highly trained and efficient, although small in number. They are not only a powerful symbol of the country but also the major safeguarders of national security, defending national interest and maintaining national stability and development. When viewed from the current conditions of building China's armed forces, although the overall scale of the military is appropriate, the structure of the forces, especially the internal structures of the services and army, is not sufficient. China must give full consideration to combat force building, keeping the incorporation of new ideas and technology as the prime focus.

First, the military should change the traditional habit of focusing on the Army, and should direct its attention toward the building of all the armed forces—the Navy, the Air Force, and the Second Artillery Force—so as to formulate combat capabilities that would satisfy the needs of IT-based warfare.

Second, the armed forces should think beyond mechanized wars. Mechanized wars are combats of iron and steel, fire, maneuver, speed, fire range of weapons as well as involve the quantity of tanks and armored weaponry. However, future IT-based warfare, although still essentially involving blood and fire best demonstrated by large-scale fire strikes, will have altered forms of combat. Wars will change from traditional modes to non-contact, non-linear, and asymmetric warfare. This will put more emphasis on the integration of mechanized combat platforms through the flow of information in a bid to realize long-distance and accurate combat. Further, it will focus more on the integration of intelligence, information, and command control during combat, emphasizing that the mechanized combat platform can release greater combat effectiveness.

Third, the armed forces must look toward integrated development rather than isolated development by establishing their own system among the services and arms. In the past, as the source of threats to China's integrity mainly came via land-based invasions, the Navy, Air Force, and Second Artillery Force served as coordinators, each administering its own methods. However, the battle space of futuristic IT-based warfare will not be restricted to one-dimensional, two-dimensional, or three-dimensional spaces; rather, it will be a multi-dimensional sphere of land, sea, air, space, and electronics. Hence, the role of sea, air, space, and electronic supremacy is becoming increasingly

Informatization building of the armed forces is first on all top agendas related to military construction.

important, requiring the combat forces of the services and arms to establish seamless links aimed at inter-exchange and inter-connection. Thus, it is necessary for the combat forces to steadily reduce the differences among the different services and arms and enhance their integration so as to formulate integrated joint combat capabilities.

Fourth, while giving full consideration to the combat force building of services and arms, it is imperative that the combat forces adhere to coordinated planning and integrated advancement. IT-based warfare is no longer an individual confrontation of the combat unit, but a system confrontation based on the integration of various combat units and combat elements.

Thus, China will stick to scientific proof and will integrate planning and top-level design, adopting strong and forceful measures for step-by-step implementation and overall advancement. It should formulate designs and plans targeting the building of the services and arms as a whole. In line with the country's economic strength and scientific and technological level, and with the coordinated development of the nation's economic construction, the armed forces should design scientific and reasonable building guidelines and

The Navy carries out combat drills and exercises to enhance the troops' rapid reaction and integrated logistics support capabilities.

principles so as to avoid aiming too high and being too impatient for success. By closely focusing on the requirement of integrated joint combat, the military should readjust the current ratio and structure of the services and arms, and formulate a system of armed forces and a mode of coordinated development with information and intelligence as the leading factor, nuclear strike power as the deterrent force, long distance and accurate strike as the pillar, ground combat force as the basis, air and naval forces as the focus, and with militia and reserved forces as the backing. The armed forces should gradually change the current track of vertical independent development by the services and arms, and advance toward horizontal integration of the services and arms, informatization digitalization as well as the integration of the

Military parade, held on October 1, 2009 in Beijing to mark the 60th anniversary of the founding of the People's Republic of China.

armed forces. The country should gradually build and improve the combat forces with mutual reliance and mutual supplement of the services and arms, enhance the building of joint combat command system, and steadily promote the reform of combat support system and elevate comprehensive support capabilities.

Giving Full Consideration to Current and Long-term Development

National defense and armed forces building is a process of steady change and development. Thus, in the building of national defense and armed forces, China should focus on doing a good job with an eye on the future, and give full consideration to current and long-term development so as to ensure the sustainable development of national defense and the armed forces.

China needs to give full consideration to the planning of current and long-term development. The armed forces should formulate plans coordinating current and long-term development. It should strengthen overall planning and do a good job in top-level design in a bid to establish the long-term, mid-term, and short-term objective of national defense and armed forces development. In formulating designs and plans, the armed forces

THE OVERALL REQUIREMENT OF IMPLEMENTING SCIENTIFIC OUTLOOK ON NATIONAL DEVELOPMENT

- To adhere to the fundamental principle of the Party exercising absolute leadership over the armed forces and the fundamental nature and purpose of the armed forces serving the people and to comprehensively strengthen the building to make the armed forces more revolutionary, modernized, and standardized
- To effectively carry out the historical missions of the armed forces at this new stage in the new century, and enhance the deterrence and combat capabilities within IT-based conditions as the fundamental starting point and final goal
- To ensure coordination between the revolution in military affairs with Chinese characteristics and preparations for military struggle, mechanization and informatization, building of combat forces in services and arms, current and long-term development, and efforts devoted to the main and secondary strategic directions.
- To further implement the strategy of building a strong armed force through science and technology; to promote innovation in military theory, technology, organization, and management; to speed up the change in the mode of generating combat capabilities
- To give full play to the main role of the large mass of officers and soldiers, maintain the integration of military economy and civilian economy and combine military efforts with civilian support so as to realize the comprehensive, balanced and sustainable development of national defense and building of the armed forces

should not only consider the current construction but also keep an eye on long-term development so as to pursue overall consideration and coordinated development.

The military should combine and coordinate the current and long-term development of the armed forces by integrating current structure and preparedness for realistic military struggle into the long-term development of national defense and armed forces, use the partial leapfrogging of military struggle preparedness to promote the comprehensive and coordinated development of national defense and armed forces building, and use the overall long-term development objectives to lead the current building of national defense and armed forces. The military should plan the building of national defense and armed forces from the longer term point of view, and strive to achieve high-level joint combat capabilities under IT-based conditions. The armed forces should not only meet the country's security needs in the near future but also meet the nation's long-term security needs so as to realize the unity between current construction and long-term development.

By basing itself on the current conditions, and following scientific laws, the armed forces should correctly handle the objective requirement and realistic possibilities, make progress while leaving some things as they are, highlight the focuses, do what is possible and seek steady advancement, so as to put limited resources on the major orientation and key links of military struggle, and achieve the best results in construction.

Chapter 4

China's Armed Forces and Its Historic Mission

The armed forces is an umbrella term that encompasses all the armed groups in a country and is a major component of a country's state power as well as a key reflection of the strength of the country. If we take a sweeping look at world history, the prosperity and development of a country all depend on strong armed forces to provide reliable security guarantee. The armed forces of the People's Republic of China (PRC) are composed of the People's Liberation Army (PLA), the reserve forces, and the Chinese People's Armed Police Force. China is dedicated to building armed forces that are commensurate with its own status and adapting to the interest of its national development.

China's Leadership and Administration System for its Armed Forces

In accordance with the Constitution and the National Defense Law, the National People's Congress (NPC) of the PRC, which is the highest level of state power, is the sole decider on whether to engage in war and general or partial mobilization. The president of the state, in accordance with the decisions of the NPC and its Standing Committee, proclaims a state of war and issues mobilization orders. The State Council directs and administers national defense work. Since 1982, the Communist Party of China (CPC) and the PRC have jointly set up the Central Military Commission (CMC), and established the highest military leadership system in which the CPC and the state jointly assume leadership. The CPC Central Committee has supreme leadership on the country's armed forces.

Under the direct leadership of the CMC, the leading cadres of China's armed forces are composed of four general headquarters and departments of the PLA, military area commands, and other units.

The CMC

CMC members include the chairman, the vice-chairmen, and others. The Chairman of the CMC is responsible for the commission. Its offices are the PLA's General Staff Headquarters, General Political Department, General Logistics Department, and General Armaments Department. Through the four general headquarters and departments, the CMC exercises operational command over the whole PLA and leadership for the development of the PLA.

The Four General Headquarters and Departments

The General Staff Department is the leading organ responsible for military work of the country's armed forces. It organizes and directs the development of China's armed forces, and organizes and commands their military operations. Under it are departments in charge of operations, intelligence, communications, electronic countermeasures (ECM), military training and arms, adjutant and force structure, mobilization, army aviation, foreign affairs, management, and so on.

The General Political Department is the leading organ responsible for the political work of China's armed forces. It administers the armed forces' Party work and organizes their political work. Under it are departments in charge of Party affairs, personnel, publicity, security, discipline inspection, civil-military affairs, and so on.

The General Logistics Department is the leading organ responsible for the logistical work of China's armed forces. It administers the logistical construction and logistical support work of the armed forces. Under it are departments in charge of financial matters, quartermaster materials and petroleum, oils, and lubricants, health administration, military transportation, capital construction and barracks, auditing, and so on. The General Armaments Department is the leading organ responsible for the equipment of China's armed forces. It administers the provision of equipment for the armed forces. Under it are departments in charge of overall planning, equipment for all services and arms, procurement for Army's military equipment R&D, general purpose equipment support, electronic information infrastructure, equipment and technological cooperation, and so on.

Units under the Direct Leadership of the CMC

The Academy of Military Sciences (AMS) is the PLA's highest-level research institute under the direct leadership of the CMC and center of military science research of the PLA.

The National Defense University (NDU) is the PLA's highest military institution of higher learning under the direct leadership of the CMC, mainly responsible for the education and training of senior commanding and staff officers and senior researchers, as well as local senior- and medium-level cadres.

The National University of Defense Technology (NUDT) is a comprehensive university under the direct leadership of the CMC, mainly responsible for the education and training of senior scientists and engineers, and specialized commanding officers, as well as conducting research on national defense science and technology.

The People's Liberation Army (PLA)

The PLA, the principal body of China's armed forces, has a total strength of 2,300,000. The PLA is mainly responsible for conducting defense-related operations under IT-based conditions, and, if necessary, helping to maintain social order in accordance with the law.

The Army

The PLA, which was established on August 1, 1927, is primarily responsible for land-based military operations. At present, the Army has no independent leading organ, and the functions of the leading organ are exercised by the four general headquarters or departments. The seven military area commands, namely, those of Shenyang, Beijing, Lanzhou, Jinan, Nanjing, Guangzhou, and Chengdu, exercise direct leadership over the Army units under their command. The Army has such arms as infantry, armor, artillery, air defense, Army aviation, engineering, chemical defense, and communications, as well as other specialized units such as those of the ECM, reconnaissance, and mapping.

The infantry—maneuvering and operating on foot, in armored personnel carriers, or infantry fighting vehicles—is composed of mountain infantry,

The armored corps (tank corps) of the Army.

motorized infantry, and mechanized infantry (armored infantry). The infantry is mainly equipped with close combat weapons, which are lightweight and convenient to carry and operate, including various types of small arms, light artillery, and anti-tank weapons. Motorized infantry is equipped with various types of personnel carriers, which are easy to maneuver.

Armored infantry tanks of the PLA Army pass a pontoon.

Mechanized infantry is equipped with multi-type, home-made infantry fighting vehicles and armored personnel carriers.

The armored corps (tank corps)—equipped with tanks and other armored vehicles and support vehicles—carries out ground assaults. Their equipment includes multi-type main battle tanks, amphibious tanks, mine-sweeping tanks, and renaissance tanks, as well as operation and logistics support vehicles covering infantry fighting vehicles, armored personnel carriers, self-propelled guns, armored reconnaissance vehicles, and armored command cars.

The artillery corps—equipped with artillery for suppression and anti-tank purposes, and missiles for anti-tank and other operational-tactical purposes—carries out ground fire strikes. Their equipment includes multi-caliber cannons, howitzers, canon howitzers, rocket launchers, mortars, smoothbore and recoilless guns, as well as the "Red Arrow" series anti-tank missile.

The air defense corps—equipped with anti-aircraft artillery and ground-to-air missile systems—carries out ground-to-air operations.

The Army aviation corps—equipped with attack, transport, and other specialized helicopters and light fixed-wing aircraft—carries out air maneuvers and provide support for ground operations. They are mainly equipped with transport or attack helicopters, and armed or multi-purpose helicopters.

Transport helicopter fleet of the Army aviation corps.

The engineering corps—responsible for engineering support—is composed of engineering and other specialized units of pontoons, construction, camouflage, field water supply, and engineering maintenance. Their equipment mainly includes engineering detection equipment, mine laying and clearance equipment, river-crossing and bridge equipment, engineering machinery, camouflage equipment, tools and other equipment.

The chemical defense corps, responsible for chemical defense operations, is composed of chemical defense, flame-throwing and smoke-generating units. Their equipment mainly includes nuclear explosion observation equipment, radiation detection equipment, chemical detection equipment, decontamination vehicles, flame-throwing, and smoke-generating equipment.

The communications corps, responsible for military communications, is composed of specialized units engaged in communications, communications engineering, communications technical support, aviation navigation, and military postal service. They are equipped with multi-modeled communications and automatic command facilities covering radio, single sideband radio, ultra-short wave relay, carrier telephone, and communication receivers.

Corps for ECM are specialized units capable of launching electronic attack and defense, and are equipped with various types of electronic equipment.

The Army's reconnaissance corps march with light packs

Reconnaissance corps are specialized units with military intelligence, and are equipped with various types of reconnaissance equipment and light and rapid transport vehicles.

Mapping corps shoulder military mapping tasks and are equipped with such advanced equipment as GPS positioning instruments, theodolite instruments, digital mapping GPS, and geodesy car. They are also divided into field mobile, sea border defense, frontier defense, and garrison troops.

Currently, the field mobile troops of the Army have 18 combined corps, and some independent combined operational divisions and brigades. The organizational order of the field mobile troops is normally combined corps, division (brigade), regiment, battalion, company, platoon, and squad. The organizational systems of the sea border defense, frontier defense, and garrison troops are decided in accordance with their operational tasks and geographical conditions.

The institutions training the Army's qualified professionals mainly include the Shijiazhuang Army Command College, Nanjing Army Command College, Shijiazhuang Mechanized Infantry Academy, Xi'an Army Institute, and Nanchang Army Institute. In addition, there are some arms technology institutions training qualified professionals for the Army's armored corps, anti-tank missile corps, artillery corps, Army aviation corps, air defense corps, mapping corps, chemical defense corps, and engineering corps.

The Navy

The Navy was established on April 23, 1949 as a strategic service of the PLA. Its primary missions are, independently or jointly with the Army and Air Force, to guard against enemy invasion from the sea, defend the state's sovereignty over its territorial waters, and safeguard the state's maritime rights and interests. The Navy has such arms as the submarine, surface, naval aviation, coastal defense, and marine corps as well as other specialized units. Under the Navy, there are three fleets, namely, the Beihai, Donghai, and Nanhai fleets. Each fleet supervises fleet detachments and air divisions.

The submarine force is composed of both conventional and nuclear-powered units, with underwater attack and some nuclear counterattack capabilities, respectively. The nuclear-powered submarine force, which assumes the strategic nuclear counterattack mission, is under the direct command of the CMC. China's Navy is equipped with multi-modeled conventionally powered submarines carrying such weapons as torpedoes, sea mines, cruise missiles, and ballistic missiles. The nuclear submarine force is equipped with nuclear attack submarines and ballistic missile nuclear submarines, with the former carrying torpedoes and cruise missiles as major weapons, and the latter carrying strategic nuclear weapons, which are the major components of China's strategic nuclear forces.

Conventional submarine fleet conducting drills.

The surface combat force is equipped with multi-type destroyers, frigates, missile boats, torpedoes, hunting submarines, mine-laying boats, mine-sweeping vessels, landing ships, and hovercrafts, while the ship is equipped with weapons such as small and medium-caliber guns, ship-to-ship missiles, anti-submarine weapons, and ship-to-air missiles. In particular, destroyers and frigates are the main warships, and all are equipped with missiles, with some able to land helicopters. The surface support force is equipped with carriers, oil tankers, water boats, refrigerated ships, engineering ships, degaussing ships, hospital ships, lifeboats, and reconnaissance ships.

The naval aviation force is composed of bomber, fighter-bomber, attacker, fighter, anti-submarine and reconnaissance units, and security, ECM, transport, rescue, and air refueling units, which have reconnaissance, security, anti-ship, antisubmarine, and air defense capabilities. The naval aviation is equipped with multi-typed fighters, medium-range bombers, fighter-bombers, seaplanes, reconnaissance aircraft, anti-submarine aircraft, transport planes and ship-based helicopters. Airborne weapons include air guns, air rockets, aviation bombs, air-to-air missiles, air-to-ship missiles, torpedoes, and deep-water bombs.

The naval coastal defense force is composed of shore-to-ship missile and coastal artillery units, which have capabilities to defend China's coasts. It is equipped with mobile and fixed shore-to-ship cruise missiles and large-caliber automated shore artillery.

Missic destroyer fleet.

The marine corps has infantry, artillery, armor, and engineering units, as well as reconnaissance, chemical defense, and communications units. It is a rapid assault force for amphibious operations, and has developed into a quick reaction force that incorporates many arms and has many ground, maritime, and underwater operation capabilities, being dubbed as "a fierce tiger on the ground, a huge dragon in the sea, and a powerful eagle in the air." It is mainly equipped with various types of landing ships, high-speed landing ships and hovercraft, amphibious tanks and armored vehicles, as well as other various automated firearms and equipment suiting amphibious operations.

The institutions training the Navy's qualified professionals mainly include the Naval Command College, Naval Engineering University, Naval Submarine College, Dalian Naval Academy, and Guangzhou Naval Academy.

The Air Force

As a strategic service of the PLA, the Air Force was established on November 11, 1949. Its primary missions are organizing homeland air defense to protect airspace and providing air security for key facilities; organizing relatively independent air

A new fighter of the Air Force aviation corps.

offensive operations; independently or jointly with the Army, Navy, or Second Artillery Force, engaging in joint operations against enemy invasion from the air, or conducting air strikes against the enemy. Adopting a system of combining aviation with ground-to-air defense forces, the Air Force consists of the aviation, surface-to-air missile, anti-aircraft artillery and airborne units, as well as communications, radar, ECM, chemical defense, technical reconnaissance, and other specialized units. The Air Force has an air command in each of the seven military areas of Shenyang, Beijing, Lanzhou, Jinan, Nanjing, Guangzhou, and Chengdu. In the major direction and target zones, there are air corps or corps-level air bases.

The aviation is composed of fighter, attacker, bomber, reconnaissance, transport and support units, usually in the organizational order of division, regiment, group, and squadron. An aviation division generally has under its command two to three aviation regiments and related stations. The aviation regiment is the basic tactical unit.

The fighter force is equipped with multi-typed fighters with airborne weapons including air cannons, air rockets, aviation bombs, and air-to-air missiles. The attacker force is equipped with medium-range bombers that can carry conventional bombs, air-to-ground missiles, and nuclear missiles. The bomber force is equipped with multi-typed bombers with airborne weapons including air cannons, air rockets, aviation bombs, and air-to-ground missiles. The reconnaissance force is equipped with multi-typed tactical reconnaissance aircraft with airborne equipment including various types of large, medium, and small-sized transport aircraft and helicopters. In addition, the aviation force is also equipped with specialized aircraft such as ECM aircraft, air command and early warning aircraft, and air refueling aircraft.

The Air Force dispatching large transport aircraft with airdrop relief supplies to quake-hit (inaccessible) areas in Sichuan Province, May 22, 2008.

The ground-to-air missile force and anti-aircraft artillery force are usually organized into divisions (brigades), regiments, battalions, and companies, who are equipped with ground-to-air missiles, automatic anti-aircraft systems and supporting radar systems. The ground-to-air missile force has established a strong defense system in low, medium, and high altitudes, with short-range, medium-range, and long-range weapons that can combat aircraft and intercept cruise missiles in China's vast airspace.

The airborne force is mainly based in China's central regions, and is organized into corps, divisions, regiments, battalions, and companies. They have highly mobile emergency response capabilities and combat effectiveness, and when necessary, they can deploy these to any part of China within several hours or a dozen hours in organic units to conduct missions. They are equipped with mobile tools such as large and medium-sized transport aircraft and various types of parachutes, as well as weapons ranging from infantry light weapons, mortars, recoilless guns, anti-aircraft machine guns, rockets, and howitzers.

With radar as basic equipment, the radar force is organized into brigade (regiment), battalion, and company, carrying out missions of air target reconnaissance and air situation reports. At present, the radar force has established a radar pre-warning network covering the whole nation, playing a vital role in aspects such as safeguarding the homeland and anti-aircraft defense, flight control, operations, and flight training of the aviation corps. The radar force is mainly equipped with multi-typed over-the-horizon, ultra-long range, medium and long-range, medium and short-range warning radars, as well as many types of directing radars.

The institutions training the Air Force's qualified professionals mainly include the Air Force Command Academy, the Air Force Engineering University, the Air Force Institute of Aviation, the Air Force Radar Academy, and the Air Force Institute of Logistics.

The Second Artillery Force

As a strategic force under the direct leadership of the CMC, the Second Artillery Force was established on July 1, 1966. It is composed of the ground-to-ground strategic nuclear missile force, the conventional operational-tactical missile force, and the support units, and is organized into missile base, brigade, and battalion.

The strategic nuclear missile force, under the direct command of the CMC, constitutes the main part of China's limited nuclear counterattack capability of certain size and with war-fighting capabilities. Its primary missions are to deter the enemy from using nuclear weapons against China, and, in the case of a nuclear attack by the enemy, to launch an effective counterattack in self-defense independently or jointly with the strategic nuclear forces of other services, at the order of the supreme command.

The conventional operational-tactical missile force is equipped with conventional operational and tactical missile systems. Its task is to carry out fire assaults with conventional missiles. It is equipped with the "Dongfeng" series of medium and long-range missiles and intercontinental ballistic missiles, which have gradually realized solid (fuel) upgrading, mobility and small size improvement, developed various types of launch modes and warheads so as to enhance precision strike capabilities, rapid response capabilities, penetration capabilities, and destroying capabilities.

The conventional operational-tactical missile force is equipped with conventional operational and tactical missile systems, and carries out fire assaults with conventional missiles. The Second Artillery Force is focusing on developing a major conventional combat force so as to win local wars under IT-based conditions while further enhancing the force's nuclear counterattack capability. It is mainly equipped with short-range ballistic missiles and China-made new-typed ground-to-ground cruise missiles, and can launch deep conventional assaults independently or jointly with the other services and arms, having precision strike capabilities. As China's major nuclear counterattack force, the Second Artillery Force strictly implements the Chinese government's commitment to the world: China develops limited nuclear weapons, which are solely aimed at breaking nuclear monopoly, opposing nuclear

Anti-aircraft missile launches.

blackmail against it, and enhancing self-defense; containing possible nuclear attacks so as to defend national security and safeguard world peace. China will not be the first to use nuclear weapons and will not take part in a nuclear arms race nor will it deploy nuclear weapons in foreign countries. China implements strict management on nuclear weapons, nuclear technology, and nuclear materials, and there is a reliable guarantee for China's nuclear safety.

The institutions training the Second Artillery Force's qualified professionals mainly include the Second Artillery Engineering College and the Second Artillery Command College.

National Defense Reserve Force

The militia is a mass armed force engaged in daily production; it is the reserve force of the PLA, and the basis of a people's war. Mao Zedong said that "the most profound root of the great power of war lies in the people." Army and civilians are the foundation of victory. During the Chinese Revolutionary War, in cooperating with regular troops in combat, the Chinese militia carried out memorable feats for the emancipation of the Chinese nation and the founding of New China. After the founding of the People's Republic of China in 1949, the militia has played an important role in the struggle to build and defend the motherland. In the new era after 1978, in accordance with the stipulations of the National Defense Law, the General Staff Headquarters administers the building of the militia under the leadership of the State Council and the CMC.

Under the command of the military organs, the militia in wartime helps the standing army in its military operations, conducts independent operations, and provides combat support and manpower replenishment for the standing army. During peacetime, it undertakes the tasks of performing combat readiness support, taking part in emergency rescue and disaster relief efforts, and maintaining social order. In accordance with the provisions of the Military Service Law of the PRC, a selected group of militiamen under the age of 28, including soldiers discharged from active service and other persons who have received or are selected for military training, shall be regimented into the primary militia; other male citizens belonging to the age group of 18 to 35 years, who are qualified for reserve service, shall be regimented into the ordinary militia. The age limit for primary militiamen may be extended appropriately in frontier areas on land or sea, areas inhabited by minority nationalities as well as urban units in special circumstances. The primary militiamen are Class A reserves, while ordinary militiamen are Class B reserves. Rural towns and townships, administrative villages, urban sub-districts, and enterprises and institutions of a certain scale are the basic units in which the militia is

Anti-aircraft artillery unit of the reserve force.

organized. Militiamen in an administrative village are generally organized into militia company (battalion), while the primary militiamen are organized independently. To ensure that militiamen are always ready to respond to the call in case of contingency, the Chinese government has formulated a militia combat readiness system, whereby combat readiness education is carried out regularly among the militia with the purpose of enhancing their national defense awareness, and exercises are conducted in accordance with combat readiness plans to enhance the militia's operational capabilities.

In principle, the people's armed forces department in the county (city, district) implements military training for primary militiamen and ordinary militiamen. In accordance with the requirement of the training outline, officers shall receive military training for 30 to 40 days each year, while militiamen shall receive military training for 15 days each year. The period of training for professional and technical militiamen may be extended appropriately according to actual needs. At present, China has set up large numbers of county-level militiamen training bases, and professional and technical militiamen training centers. Military training for militiamen can be largely conducted in the bases in a concentrated manner.

The PLA's reserve force, established in 1983, is a force with its own preset organizational structure, with reserve personnel as the base and active personnel as the backbone, and it is an important reserve force composed of Army, Navy, Air Force, and Second Artillery Force reserve forces or units. The reserve force operates a unified organizational system. The divisions, brigades, and regiments of the reserve force are conferred designations and military banners. The reserve force implements orders and regulations of the PLA, and is incorporated into the PLA's order of battle. During peacetime, it is led by the provincial military districts or garrison commands, and in wartime, after mobilization, it is commanded by the designated active unit or carries out combat missions independently. It receives military training in peacetime in accordance with the relevant regulations, and, if necessary, helps to maintain social order in accordance with the law. In wartime, it may be called into active service in pursuance of a state mobilization order. The formation of reserve forces is an important measure in implementing rapid mobilization in an organic formation, enhancing the quality of reserves, saving military expenditures, and strengthening national defense building.

The People's Armed Police Forces

The Chinese people's armed police forces, consisting of internal security forces and the gold mine, forest, water conservancy, electricity power, and transportation forces, was set up on June 19, 1982. Other forces incorporated in the armed police forces include frontier, fire, and garrison forces.

The armed police forces can be divided into three categories according to the tasks they perform:

The first category is the internal security forces. Being the main body of the Chinese people's armed police forces, the internal security forces consist of contingents and mobile divisions that receive direct leadership from the general headquarters. The tasks of the armed police forces include performing guard duties at fixed points and armed patrol in cities, guaranteeing the safety of the country's key points, dealing with contingencies, and safeguarding national security and social stability.

The second category includes the gold mine, forest, water conservancy, electricity power, and transportation forces. These forces also take orders from

The armed police salute the squadron.

the general headquarters and are supervised by relevant departments of the State Council. They not only receive tasks of economic construction but also safeguard national security and social stability. The third category includes the frontier, fire, and garrison forces, of which the frontier forces mainly undertake tasks of border inspection and management and offshore anti-smuggling activities; the fire forces mainly undertake tasks of fire control and fire extinction; and the garrison forces mainly perform guard duties for leaders of the Party and the country, main leaders of provinces and cities, and important visiting guests. These forces are incorporated in the armed police forces and are led by the public security departments.

The basic tasks of the armed police forces are safeguarding national security and social stability, guaranteeing the safety of key national points, lives, and people's property, and assisting the PLA in defensive combat during wartime.

The armed police force is subordinate to the State Council, and is under the dual leadership of the State Council and the CMC. It receives unified leadership and management, and its command is delegated to a relevant organ at each level. The armed police force has three echelons of leadership, namely, general headquarters, contingent (division), and detachment (regiment). The general headquarters, as the chief commanding organ of the armed police force, commands and administers internal security forces, and gold mine, forest, water conservancy, electricity power, and transportation forces. In the nationwide administrative hierarchy, the armed police contingents, detachments, and squadrons are instituted at province, prefecture, and county levels, respectively. When performing a public security task or relevant work, the armed police force unit is subordinate to the leadership and command of the public security organs at the same level.

During peacetime, the tasks of the armed police force include performing guard duties at fixed points, dealing with contingencies, combating terrorism, and supporting national economic development. It is specifically responsible for protecting and guarding state-designated objects, important visiting foreign dignitaries, leading organs of the Party and government at and above the provincial level, embassies and consulates of foreign countries in China, important national and international conferences, and sites of large-scale cultural and

The Hubei Provincial Corps of the Chinese Armed Police Force conduct anti-terrorism military drills, March 23, 2009.

sports activities. It is also responsible for posting peripheral armed guards at prisons and detention houses; providing armed protection for key departments in charge of confidential work and critical parts of important airports, radio stations, state economic departments, and national defense works, as well as important bridges and tunnels along trunk railway lines, and specially designated large road bridges. Further, it is involved in performing armed patrol and other security duties in state-designated large and medium-sized cities or specific zones. Dealing with contingencies chiefly means handling, according to law, sudden illegal incidents endangering state security or social order such as revolts, riots, and disturbances, fights with weapons, and other group activities that endanger public security. Combating terrorism chiefly means performing anti-attack, anti-hijacking, and anti-explosion tasks. Supporting national economic development chiefly means gold mine prospecting, preventing and fighting forest fires, participation in key state energy and transportation projects, and emergency rescue and disaster relief in cases of serious calamities.

The Historical Mission of the Chinese Armed Forces for the New Stage in the 21st Century

The historical mission of the armed forces refers to the basic tasks and major responsibilities during a specific historical period. It objectively reflects the characteristics of the period and developments related to national benefit and also reflects concrete military function. To summarize, the basic elements of the military mission include resisting foreign aggression, safeguarding the country's sovereignty, territorial integrity and safety, and preserving national unity and security.

The focuses of the Chinese army differed during various historical periods. During wartime before the establishment of New China, the military mission was to resist foreign aggression, struggle for national independence and liberation, and establish a state power under the people's democracy. After 1949, the armed forces became an important part of the state power apparatus. Its main mission was to safeguard the achievements of people's liberation and national construction, and national sovereignty and territorial integrity. Its mission was also to strengthen national defense, resist aggression, defend the motherland, safeguard people's work, and participate in national reconstruction since by the end of the 1970s. During the early part of the 21st century, the construction of the country and the armed forces entered a new stage, and the army also undertook a new historic mission. The armed forces should provide a guarantee for strengthening the state power led by the Chinese Communist Party, strongly safeguard the safety of the important strategic opportunity for the country's development, provide strategic support for safeguarding the country's benefit in the new era, and play an important role in safeguarding world peace and promoting common development.

The historic mission of the Chinese armed forces springs from and builds on the previous historic mission. Based on the tremendous changes in the international strategy pattern and the new safety environment in China and with an aim to safeguard the country's existence and development, the historical mission is set up to realize the great revival of the Chinese nationality and the economic and social development of the country and meet requirements of the new era.

Great changes have been taking place in the modern world, and the reform and development of modern China has also entered a key era. On the one hand, China has, on found a road to sustainable development; on the other hand, because of the changes in the international strategic patterns and the increase in the Chinese force, China might be forced to get involved in new worldwide systematic and group wars. However, wars that involve people across the whole country are not likely to happen. Economic globalization provides the necessary external capital, professionals, markets, and resources for China's development. The modern information technology revolution not only poses challenges but also provides new driving forces, energies, and

Commanders and soldiers of the Sichuan Reserve Anti-aircraft Artillery Division transport quake relief food and material to people at quake-hit areas, May 13, 2008.

The Chinese armed forces take on the responsibilities of safeguarding national security, disaster relief, and emergency fighting.

technological foundation for a historic jump in Chinese technology. China is now facing unprecedented development opportunities. Grasping and safeguarding these opportunities, realizing the modernization and the great revival of the Chinese nationality, enhancing people's welfare and ensuring that these opportunities are not impacted, interrupted, and lost are in the best interests of the country in the new era. Safeguarding the best interests is undoubtedly the lofty mission of the Chinese armed forces.

As economic globalization progresses, the Chinese economy develops closer and closer ties with the world economy. On the one hand, national interests have continuously expanded to encompass the land and the sea, space, and electromagnetic spaces, which requires greater safeguarding; on the other hand, the center of national interests shifts from survival interests to developmental ones, asking the armed forces to pay special attention to and firmly adhere to the national development interests, and create a peaceful international environment and harmonious social environment for national development when safeguarding survival interests. This is the new meaning of the historic mission of the armed forces in the new stage of the new era.

World peace and development are indispensable to China, and in return, China's peace and development makes great contributions to that of the world. The new trend and tasks demand that the Chinese armed forces make new contributions toward world peace and common development. At present and for some time to come, the Chinese armed forces should solve the contradictions between the level of modernization and winning information-based local wars, and that between the military capabilities and the historic mission in the new era. In addition, efforts should also be made to accelerate the promotion of special military changes, make full preparations for military conflicts, strengthen the day-to-day training, and ensure that the armed forces are capable of responding to crisis, safeguarding peace, and deterring and winning wars.

Chapter 5

The People's War-based Active Defense Strategy

Along with the national defense policies, China pursues active defensive military strategic policies as well. Based on winning wars under information-oriented conditions and continuing with the strategy of people's wars, the Chinese armed forces should adopt comprehensive means to actively defend and reduce crisis, and deter conflicts and wars, by closely combining military struggles with political, economic, diplomatic, cultural, and legal endeavors. The Chinese armed forces will act in self-defense and win wars in case they are unavoidable.

The Strategies of People's Wars

People's wars are the products of the Chinese people's struggle for national independence and liberation led by the Chinese Communist Party (CCP). Mao Zedong once pointed out "it is people who are the actual forces in creating world history." He also stated that "the richest source of power to wage war lies in the masses of the people," and that "the army and the people are the foundations of victory." These statements are in accord with the historical materialist point of view and the theoretical foundation of the people's war. Since the founding of the People's Republic of China (PRC), the Chinese people have become the real masters of their country. In keeping with the idea of people building up national defense, a strong national defense system is set up by firmly relying on the people and adhering to the principles of combining peacetime with wartime, integrating the army with the people, and having

STRATEGIC THINKING IN PEOPLE'S WAR

- Fighting for the fundamental interests of the masses
- Trusting and relying on the masses to the maximum
- Mobilizing, organizing, and arming the masses and fighting with them under the leadership of the Party
- Establishing a people's army
- Formulating a system of armed forces composed of the PLA, the national defense reserve forces, and the People's Armed Police Force
- Trying to win a war by combining the form of armed struggle suiting the actual need with the struggle of various forms in all fronts, and utilizing the flexible strategies and tactics

reserve soldiers among the people. Wholeheartedly relying on the masses is the greatest advantage of national defense.

The advancements in technology ensure that the structure and forms of warfare will change completely. Irrespective of how wars change, the concept of the people's war will remain and continue to occupy a place of significance.

Information-based wars do not change the nature of war. Wide application of information-based weapons only changes the form of wars. In future, China will face a series of wars—just wars that safeguard national safety, and integrity of territory and sovereignty; national interest and strategic stability; national dignity; and important development opportunities. Just wars have the support of the masses and sympathy of people all over the world. Rightness is the true nature of the people's war, and it is also an important political factor and condition through which the people's war wins. Unjust wars, on the other hand, are undoubtedly opposed by the masses. Unjust wars are also resisted and condemned by the international society.

Information-based wars must rely on the participation of the masses. They provide new space for the development of the people's war. Although the masses played various roles in the information-based wars, the nature of the roles will never change. Information-based wars have a closer relationship with politics, economy, culture, and society. The line of separation between soldiers and common people, front and rear areas, and military actions and

Military medical personnel work at quake-hit areas. The close relationship between the army and the people is the fundamental guarantee to launching the people's wars.

unmilitary ones has become more blurred. Soldiers participate in wars, but people also, directly or indirectly, participate in many aspects related to wars. Information-based wars have stretched the battlefield into multidimensional space, which includes the land, sea, air, outer space, and electron. As technology advances, more and more materials get consumed. Unremitting efforts should be made to mobilize and organize people at all fronts. Great efforts must be made to increase production, support the army, and create favorable conditions for success.

Although the basic idea of the people's war has not changed, it is necessary to research new methods and technologies. In the case of information-based wars, in particular, efforts should be made to research new methods to apply or strengthen according to the characteristics of the information-based wars. National scientific and technological innovative ability should be enhanced; development of weapons should mostly be based on information, science, and technology; and modernized and information-based weapons equipment should be developed. Innovation involving independent strategies should be realized. Efforts should ensure that countermeasures are available whenever wars take place and wherever enemies attack. The basic idea of the people's war will never be outdated as long as wars occur. Defeating the enemy requires us to trust and rely on the masses and mobilize and organize people.

The Active Defense Policy

China maintains an active defense policy, which mainly includes two aspects:

First, in nature, active defense adopts the policy of striking only after the enemy has struck. It is not aggressive and does not anticipate enemies. China will not launch an active attack unless defied by external armed forces or unless its national interest is infringed upon. China's military forces will not constitute a threat to any other country. Therefore, China passively accepts battles in terms of its military strategies. Second, the policy is active rather than passive in terms of the requirements of military actions and battles. It is essential to give full play to the initiative. Before wars, it is necessary to adopt various military methods flexibly, co-operate with political, economic, and diplomatic methods and deter wars from breaking out. In this way, nation building will not be impacted by wars. If wars are unavoidable, unremitting efforts should be made to control the scale, intensity, and process of wars and reduce the effects of wars. For this purpose, it is essential to firmly perform offensive operations during wars and restore normalcy as soon as possible. The policy of attack through defense explains the dialectical and united relationship between attack and defense; it embodies a high-level harmony between China's political and military strategies. It also gives full expression to a harmonious relationship between the characteristics of a socialist society and the autonomous self-defense military strategy, between safeguarding national security and international peace, and between rightness of the purpose of wars and firmness of maneuver.

Throughout the long-term national revolutionary wars, the Chinese Revolutionary Army has firmly held onto an active defense policy. Although great changes have taken place in the content and form of the strategic policy of the establishment of New China, the basic principle of active defense policy will never change.

In the 1950s, the early years of the PRC, Mao Zedong clearly put forward a policy of building powerful ground, air, and marine forces, and modern national defense. On March 6, 1956, Defense Minister Peng Dehuai submitted a report titled *Issues on Strategic Policies Safeguarding the Country and Building National Defense* at an extended meeting of the Central Military Commission (CMC) of the Central Committee of the CPC. In this report, New China's first "active defense" military policy was determined, which mainly answers the sudden attack by external forces at China's western costal areas.

By the end of the 1970s and 1980s, the international situation leaned toward relaxation. China began its reform and opening up. The national strategies were adjusted, and the focus of work began to shift toward economic

The offshore "Support-the-Front Guarantee" exercise.

construction. There was a strategic shift in military building too. The "active defense" policy should shift from coping with large-scale attacks at any time to possible local wars and military conflicts. On the premise of stabilizing the northern-front strategic position, unremitting efforts should be made to improve the southern front. Efforts should be made to attach importance to the ocean strategy, safeguard the state's marine rights and interest, and enhance counterattack capabilities, and the overall deterrent capability of the armed forces.

In the 1990s, the dual polar pattern disintegrated, and the international situation in general tended toward relaxation. However, there was a serious disequilibrium in the relative strength of countries. The new military reform developed rapidly, and the form of wars also changed drastically. In accordance with the international strategic pattern, the state's security environment and changes in modern warfare, China further readjusted its military strategy of active defense, making preparations for winning local wars in information-based situations. It unambiguously put forward the policy of building a strong army and striving to make the transition from a numerically superior type to a qualitatively efficient type, and from a manpower-intensive type to a technology-intensive type of armed force. Army building was quickened, and the fighting capabilities for crisis response have also been enhanced. It was a significant adjustment since the establishment of the PRC and a great development in terms of China's military strategic theory and strategic practice. As China's comprehensive strength develops and the international strategic situation changes, wars that involve the whole country are not likely to happen. However, the cause of modern wars and potential threats to China still exist. Local wars cannot be excluded. However, when information technologies develop rapidly and are widely adopted in the military field, such local wars are not traditional ones in normal conditions, but information-based ones. These local wars require more from Chinese army's defense capabilities and military strategies. Under the new conditions, in order to implement the military strategy of active defense and win information-based local wars, China particularly stresses on the following four unities. First, unity of preparing for, deterring, and winning wars is stressed. Preparing for wars is the basis, deterring wars the purpose, and winning wars the fundamental purpose. Complete and thorough preparations for wars are the sound guarantee for deterring and winning wars.

Second, efforts should be made to unify the people's war and develop information-based fighting methods. The people's war cannot be forsaken primarily because it is the core element of future success. It, however, does not mean that we can ignore military technology, especially military information technology, which plays a key role in modern times. The people's war and the information-based war cannot be regarded as contradictory. Quite the reverse: China pays great attention to the development and application of information-based operations as well as persisting in the people's war. By firmly implementing the policy of building a strong army through science and technology and seizing the opportunities of developing the atomic and hydrogen bombs and satellites, a combination of the people's war and military information technology has been realized.

Third, China has committed to the unity of strategic defense of interior lines and strategic counterattack of exterior lines. The strategic defense of interior lines aims to withstand the enemy's strike and ensure that the whole line is stable; the strategic counterattack of exterior lines is to destroy enemy means and guarantee strategic initiative. These two aspects are complementary to each other. On the premise of persisting in the strategic defense of interior lines, implementing the strategic counterattack of exterior lines is the best choice for countries that carry out defensive policies in information-based conditions. China stresses that it is essential to grasp opportunities and launch counterattacks on the enemy at the earliest. As for countermeasures, taking on the enemy actively is preferred to passive protection. As for fighting space, it is better to attack enemies as far away as possible from our own land. Efforts should be made to carry the wars into enemy territory. Fourth, unremitting efforts should be made to annihilate the enemy's effective strength and deplete the enemy's forces. In information-based conditions, annihilating the enemy's effective strength is significant to affecting the enemy's social psychology and shaking its resolve. Information-based local wars are represented by integrated opposition between different systems. Fighting should focus on destroying the structure and order of any operation, and paralyzing the enemy's operation structure, which will lay a solid foundation for winning wars.

Strategic Application of Military Forces

The PLA actively implements the strategy of active defense, persists in combined operation, and gives full play to various services and arms. Efforts should be made to win information-based local wars, answer various threats, and accomplish diverse military tasks.

Ground Force

The transition from regional defense to trans-regional mobility should be gradually carried out. Efforts should be made to enhance the air-ground network, long-distance maneuvers, fast action, and special counterattack capability.

Combined operation involving various services and arms will be the basic form of operation. In the combined operation, ground forces must not limit themselves to traditional concepts such as "land is the main battlefield"; instead, they must consider the situation as a whole, co-operate with other cadres of the armed forces, and fight actively. It is essential to give full play to direct contact with enemies and flexible operations in the battlefield. Ground forces should undertake more combined operations, actively create and grasp favorable opportunities, report war situations and information, and provide favorable conditions for other services and arms.

Ground force operation together with air and marine forces must coordinate and work toward putting up an integrated counterattack. It is necessary to give full play to comprehensive counterattack capability. Therefore, firepower and military strength, soft kills and hard attacks, and high-tech weapons and regular weapons should be brought into close association.

Ground forces should take attack and fielding into consideration, with attack as the dominant countermeasure. The command system combining attack should be established. Not only should the command organization be streamlined but also the command methods should be made automatic. The mobility and regeneration capabilities of command organizations should be enhanced to realize stable and continuous command. According to the

Soldiers seize positions on the beach.

characteristics of fighting on land, deploying combined attack and fielding should be established, air defense and deep defensive deployment at the rear areas should be enhanced, and efforts should be made to organize operations that frustrate the enemy.

Marine Force

The offshore defense of the marine force should be further developed, and the offshore marine comprehensive counterattack capability and nuclear counterattack capability should be enhanced.

Existence and development of a state's marine force is impacted by marine strategies, demands for the marine force by the military strategies, the resolve to utilize oceanic resources and the ocean theory of a nation. Any marine force that is limited by land strategies is doomed to fail. In recent years, China's marine strategies have shifted from shoreline defense to offshore defense. The military strategy of active defense also presents itself in offshore defense. Offshore defense is in nature defensive, but active in terms of actions. As for military actions whose main tasks are to safeguard marine rights and interest, the strategic initiative is extremely important for the strategic control

Chinese vessels sailing in international waters.

of remote sea areas. The navy, on the premise of obeying and serving national policies, should adapt itself to the needs of China's offshore military struggles, shifting to remote sea areas.

As the world's politics, economy, and diplomacy are more focused on maritime space, the strategic function of marine forces tends to be cross-border and unmilitary. Marine forces must co-operate with political, diplomatic, and economic means, creating favorable conditions. Application of naval strategies is more than just military action—it must pay attention to volatile international situations, develop its counterattack capability through developing marine resources and inspecting the changing situations. Application of naval strategies should take the function of unmilitary factors and serve the state's economic construction, and reform and opening up. In addition, prudence is important in weapon utilization.

Air Force

Transition from air-defense to attack-defense should be accelerated. The air strike capability, aerial defense and missile defense system, early warning and reconnaissance system, and strategic delivering capability should also be enhanced.

Given that future wars will be high-tech and information-based ones, the air force will carry out various missions in terms of military deterrence and combined operation. Strategies of air force feature "active defense and attack-defense system" and "safeguarding rights and interest and being used at the front."

Aggression and offensive operation are the basic characteristics of the air force. Therefore, "active defense and attack-defense system" is the guiding principle of air strategies. Among the state's armed forces, the air force has rapid-action capability. Air attack is an important military means for carrying out the military strategy of active defense in information-based conditions. The air force, when implementing the active defense policy, should combine strategic defense with the active attack, resistance with counterattack, and interior-line fight with exterior-line attack. The Chinese air force is one that combines aviation with ground-to-air defense. Air defense for the nation is one of its important strategic tasks. The strategic function of the air force is given full play by combining air attack with air

Chinese J-10 fighters during a performance on November 15, 2009 at Shahe Airport in suburban Beijing in celebration of the 60th anniversary of the Chinese Air Force.

defense operations, assisting air attack through defense, and protecting air defense through air attack. Enemies who attempt to encroach on China's territory are attacked to safeguard the state's safety.

According to international law and international common practice, the space covered by air strategies includes a wide range of areas, including territorial land, territorial sea, and territorial space, and the exclusive economic zone and the marine space over the continental shelf waters under national jurisdiction. Therefore, application of air force strategies should be in accord with national interest. Attack capability and construction of supporting facilities should be enhanced to realize a transition from air defense for the nation to attack-defense and the air strike capability, aerial defense and missile defense system, early warning and reconnaissance system, and strategic delivery capability should be enhanced.

The Second Artillery Force

The capacity of structures equipped with nuclear and conventional weapons should be gradually enhanced, and deterrence and conventional counterforce should also be enhanced.

Operations of the second artillery force have a close bearing on the national interest, war situation, comprehensive effects of politics, diplomacy, and military affairs, the international situation, and relations with big powers. All actions of the second artillery force are under the highly centralized command of the CMC of the Central Committee of the CPC. It will strictly carry out missions in accordance with the strategic intentions of the CMC.

The second artillery force is small in number but highly trained and can serve all purposes. The second artillery force, in accordance with the national planned policies and plans, mainly improves the quality of nuclear weapons on the premise of maintaining a certain number of weapons. In this way, it will be developed into a reliable force with a small number of, but highly trained and supporting, facilities.

The second artillery force is equipped with conventional and nuclear weapons. Great changes have taken place in the form of modern wars, in which the nuclear missile force plays a key role. Conventional missile force is also strategically important for counterattacks. To be "efficient enough," unremitting efforts should be made to enhance the capability of long-distance precision strikes and to keep a balance between the development of nuclear forces and conventional ones. In this way, the strategic and comprehensive functions of nuclear and conventional weapons are given full play. Battles can be won without being fought.

Chapter 6

China's Special Military Reform and Innovation

Given the global military reforms and the requirements of development and national safety, China has quickened its steps since the 21st century to promote its special military reform in accordance with its actual conditions. China's national defense and military building have entered a new stage.

The Modern World and the Basic Characteristics of China's New Military Reforms

Since the 1970s, human society has witnessed tremendous technological changes. People have seen a rapid development in information-based technologies. These include microelectronic technology, computer technology, artificial intelligence technology, and communication technology; aerospace technologies including man-made satellites, space shuttles, spacecrafts, space vehicles, and space stations; nuclear energy technologies such as nuclear fusion; new material technologies including composite materials and high temperature-resistant materials; and biological technologies such as genetic engineering. Further, development and application of marine resources such as ocean engineering have been widely applied to military fields and have initiated military reforms that involve the whole world and have an extensive influence. The idea of such a military reform is to realize a qualitative leap in weapon efficiency and give full support to maintain an advanced strategic position in an international strategic pattern. The basic aim of the military reform is to transform mechanical-based armed forces into information-based ones. Development of information-based technology directly results in such a military reform, and information-based construction and "system integration" are the basic measures. Finally, a new military system featured with information will be established. Informatization is the essence of new military reform. Among elements involved in wars, such as people, materials, power, and information, information has gradually become the essential element that controls other elements. The form of wars has changed and they have been transformed from mechanical to information-based ones; armed forces have also transformed into information-equipped ones. The new military reform will result in a series of changes in terms of army construction and fighting measures. Information-based weapons will

China keeps pace with global trends in the aerospace field.

The North Sea Fleet conducting a night drill.

become the key element to improve fighting capability; non-contact and non-linear fighting will be important fighting measures; system opposition will become the basic form on the battlefields; and space will become the new strategic commanding point of international military competition. Information-based military reform will have the greatest influence ever known. China's special military reform will attach great importance to informatization. It will adapt itself to the development trend of global military reform to realize the overall transformation of army building in accordance with China's situation. Efforts will be made to build a modern standardized army that can win future information-based wars.

Centering on Informatization and Pursuing Forward-leaping Development

Forward-leaping development is crucial for the promotion of military reform and the establishment of an information-based military system. Modernization of national defense and armed forces is, in nature, a concept of dynamic development. Put forward in the 1950s, the goal of national defense and armed forces modernization is mechanization. Long-term efforts in this regard have paid off today. China has made great progress in the modernization of the national defense and armed forces. Limited by economic development, semi-mechanization still dominates the Chinese armed forces. Mechanization is not yet complete, and informatization is already underway. China must realize its current situation, and not expect an overhaul in terms of mechanization and informatization. It should not follow western countries in the building of its national defense and armed forces, and mechanization and informatization should not be developed step by

Adaptability test of communication equipment.

A national defense exhibition.

step; China should give full play to every favorable opportunity and firmly adhere to the principle of increasing mechanization and informatization. Mechanization in modern times is different from that in previous years, and is closely linked with informatization. Informatization should be based on mechanization, which in return will promote development of informatization. Military building should center on informatization, and informatization will drive mechanization. Traditional mechanization and some early stages of informatization can be avoided. Local leaps forward may push the overall development of national defense and military reform. It is expected that the building of information-based armed forces will be completed by the middle of the 21st century.

In order to fulfill such a goal, China has put forward a "three stage" strategy. According to the strategy, modernization of the national defense and armed forces is an important part of the country's modernization drive. The modernization of the national defense and armed forces, which began toward the end of the 20th century and continues upto the middle of the 21st century, will be realized in three stages.

First, China will invest decades to plan the scale of the armed forces and its systematic organization, and improve its policies and regulations. This will lay a solid foundation for the modernization of the national defense and armed forces.

Second, as the country's economy develops and military expenditure increases, the quality of the armed forces will be raised in 2020. Military construction will record great progress at that time.

Third, in the middle of the 21st century, the modernization of the national defense and armed forces will be complete.

Of the three stages, the first is essential. In line with the overall planning of the country's modernization, China should take full advantage of the current opportunities and learn from the developed countries' experience in terms of military construction. China must make full use of domestic and international resources, maintain rapid development, and try to shorten the gaps between its military construction and that of the developed countries. Strength should be built for future development and for laying the foundation for the informatization of the national defense and armed forces. Leap-forward development of national defense and military construction is both necessary and possible.

The upgraded air force.

Self-innovation and Overall Transformation of Military System

Self-innovation is the main force driving the construction of the national defense and armed forces and speeding up military reform. It is also crucial for leap-forward development. China has long been building itself based on its own strategic resources, intelligence, and innovative work—the strategic principle for China to control its own fate and stand independently among the nations of the world.

The modernization of the national defense and armed forces that first began with the establishment of the PRC has made great progress. Although China has an independent modern defense system based on the latest science and technology, the system is still at a mid-point in its development due to limited military expenditure. Semi-mechanization still dominates the armed forces. The structural contradictions of the Chinese military are still evident. In particular, the proportion of the marine, air, and land forces is skewed, and informatization is in high demand. To some extent, the concept of the "great land force" has not been completely removed. Although China has created

A marine missile frigate launches an anti-ship missile.

theories on the people's war and active defense, practical application of these theories in information-based wars has long been a challenge. The main contradiction in the building of the national defense and armed forces is that China's armed forces are still unable to meet the requirements for winning information-based local wars. The military capacity cannot satisfy the requirements in the new century. China still lags behind developed countries in terms of the level of military modernization and technologies. Innovations in military theories, technologies, organizations, and management must be pushed forward. The basic prospective military theory plays a guiding role in China's military reform; military organization innovation levers the enhancement of fighting capacity and combination of human beings and weapon equipment. Innovation in military management is crucial to reduce construction cost and enhance the military system's operation efficiency. The enhancement of fighting capacity is the basic requirement to speed up military reform. Fighting capacity then becomes the basis to unify thoughts, make reform policies, and check reform progress.

Innovation in Military Theories

The establishment of modern military theories that are in line with information-based wars is of the most critical aspects of Chinese military reforms. A military reform without any innovation in corresponding military theories is not a true reform. To some extent, global military competition is one of innovation in military theories. A country with innovative military theories may steer military reform. Theories and technologies drive and are features of the modern-world military reform. These two elements are the essence of military reform and are indispensable in pushing reform forward. Innovation in military theories is rampant across the world, with new thoughts, concepts, and theories coming in thick and fast. New theories such as the all-dimension integration theory, information deterrence, and information attack and defense have infiltrated the military world. These new theories are results of information-based wars. As early as the 1990s, as new forms of wars and fighting methods began to surface in the military world, China first put forward a theory of "winning local wars with modern, especially high technologies."

In recent years, as new military reform has developed further, China has again clearly stated that military preparations should focus on winning information-based local wars. Mao Zedong's endeavors and backing have helped military theory innovations in China to break free of traditional military thoughts; renewed military strategies and thoughts; and established the all dimension-integration theory, capacity-based combined operation thought, medium-and long-distance precise operation thought

Commanders of the air force actively apply the art of war.

and high-intelligence operation thought. New concepts concerning success or failure, effectiveness, time and space, control, energy, and system have also been set up. China will further develop active defense operations and regular rules, and new ways and thoughts of combining the people's war theory with information technologies.

A lively, interactive training class.

Innovation in Military Technology

Innovation in military technology and information-based weapon systems is the key to China's special military reform. China, a country with a weak economy and technology, lags behind developed countries in military modernization. It is imperative that China develops and enhances information and technology-based military means and weapons so that it can advance in military capacity. In the 1980s, Deng Xiaoping pointed out that "China must develop its own high technologies and take up a position in the high-tech world." Upon Deng Xiaoping's urging, the "Suggestion on Following the Development of World Strategic High Technologies" put forward by Wang Dahang and three other senior scientists was approved. Discussions on the Suggestion were held by more than 200 well-known scientists from all parts of the country. On November 18, 1986, the Development Program of High Technology—the "863" Program—was approved. Important results in high-tech fields such as biology, airspace, information, energy, and new materials had been achieved since the implementation of the Program. Some projects even met international advanced standards. The "863" Program infused vitality into China's defense-related science and technology industries. The "Super 863" Program and other high-tech military technology plans came into being later on. China continues to carry out the strategy of "building a strong army through science and technology" to meet the requirements of systematic and asymmetric operations and opposition of information systems. Using self-innovation capacity as the basis for improving technology and weapon equipment, China adheres to principles of combining military efforts with civilian support, original and integrated innovations and combination of introduction, absorption, and re-innovation. Efforts have been strengthened to make breakthroughs in some basic, prospective, and strategic fields and to push self-, leap-forward, and sustainable development of high-tech weapons. China must insist on the policy of "shortening the battlefront and using the financial, material, and human resources in a concentrated way" and be aware of the rules and regulations. China must keep its eyes on the latest scientific and technological progress worldwide, speed up research and development of "two missiles and one satellite," share key world military technologies, master independent intellectual property rights, develop deterrence, and practical-war featuring new military means, and guarantee absolute or relative superiority on the battlefield. A mechanism to drive technical innovation and development of weapons against the demands of operation should be improved. Further, an index system concentrating on future development and in conformity with the principle of full consideration of the immediate and future needs and reasonability should also be set up. A system combining the efforts of the people and armed forces strives to promote a military-civilian scientific and technological innovation system. The self-innovation capacity in key technologies of national defense and weapon equipment must be enhanced, and China must possess some core defense-related technologies with independent intellectual property rights.

Innovation in Military Organization

China's special military reform is mainly marked by organization innovation and building of information-based armed forces, which are in return the policy guarantee for military reform. The term "military organization reform" implies deepening the reform of military structure to speed up information communication, realize efficient combination of human beings and weapons, and optimize operation efficiency. Countries of the world have exerted themselves to simplify military personnel, optimize military structure, shorten information circulation, simplify commanding procedures, enhance information and technology contents, transform traditional operation patterns to one featured with modularization, integration, and diversification, and change the vertical tree-like commanding system to a network-type one. China's armed forces have undergone several military reforms since the establishment of the country. In particular, Chinese arms have striven to make the transition from being a manpower-intensive type to a technology-intensive one, and from a numerically superior type to a qualitatively efficient one since the 1990s, laying a solid foundation for further innovation of military organizations.

China will solve structural contradictions that hamper military construction by bringing about military reform. Efforts will be made to lever proportions of arms, departments and arm units, and combatant and noncombatant units; establish a series of systems; and realize an overall transition of military structure. Efforts should be made to strengthen the country with talented people and trained professionals, who are strong and loyal to the country, well versed with military affairs and modern technologies, and who are capable of quick responses under high-intensity opposition. Such high-quality professionals include versatile commanding seniors, suggestion-providing talents, and S&T-related professionals at the expert level. The Chinese armed forces will live up to the mission assigned to them and win glorious victories.

Innovation in Military Management

Innovation of the military is another element that is the basis of military reform. Scientific and high efficient management plays an important role in reducing cost and enhancing the efficiency of military systems and operation capacity. Great changes have taken place in military organizations

The ASEAN and China, Japan, and Korea (10+3) Armed Forces International Quake Relief Seminar, held at Shijiazhuang Army Command College from June 10 to 14, 2008.

and management as equipment modernization has strengthened. Higher requirements are challenging military management. Strengthening management and enhancing quality and efficiency are necessary. To innovate management is to renew management concepts, enhance strategic management and management of arm units and resources, innovate management mechanism and means, and improve management quality.

Chapter 7

China's Modern Defense-related Science, Technology, and Industry System

China's defense-related science and technology industry is an important basis for the building of a modern national defense system. It is the backbone of research and development of weapons equipment, an important part of the country's advanced manufacturing industry, and the main driver of national science and technology innovation. China has been independently developing defense-related science and technology industry for a long time now, enhancing its overall level and economic benefit and promoting coordinated development of national defense and the economy. Significant achievements, marked by "two missiles and one satellite" and manned space industry, have been recorded in history and have greatly enhanced China's national defense, scientific research and development, overall national strength, and national cohesion.

The "senior ministries" reform led by the Chinese government started off in March 2008. The Industrial Bureau of Defense-Related Science and Technology Industry under the Ministry of Industry and Information Technology of the PRC is now in charge of defense-related science and technology affairs. Policies, laws, and regulations concerning defense-related science and technology are drafted or made by the Bureau. Following is a list of the tasks of the Bureau:

(1) research developing programs; coordinate research, production, and construction in national defense affairs;

(2) examine and approve the qualification of military product production;

(3) examine and verify contracts with respect to scientific research and production between the military and the producers;

(4) coordinate, supervise, and inspect execution of ordering contracts so as to ensure the production and supply of military equipment;

(5) exercise administration of the nuclear, space, aviation, shipbuilding, and weaponry industries;

(6) guide the administration of the military-related electronics sector;

(7) organize, study, and implement reform of the system of defense-related science, technology, and industry;

(8) adjust the capability, structure, and layout of the defense-related science, technology, and industry;

(9) draw up plans for investment in fixed assets with respect to defense-related science, technology, and industry, and for technical transformation and development of defense conversion technologies; further, organize the implementation of such plans; and

(10) conduct foreign exchanges and international cooperation in the field of defense-related science, technology, and industry.

Through the years of development, China has realized an independent and complete defense-related science and technology industry system embracing nuclear and aerospace technologies with the least cost. A group of talented people well versed in high-level technologies and boasting a fine style of work have been cultivated to lay a solid foundation for independent research on weapons.

The Road to Independent Innovation Development

Independent innovation is the essence and basis for the defense-related science and technology industry and is the impetus for continuous development. China's defense-related science and technology industry has independently paved the road for self-innovative development. History has shown that only when a country has its own core technologies and independent intellectual property rights can it control the fate of national development and security.

In the 1950s, the Chinese defense-related science and technology industry started from scratch. Workers involved in the industry worked diligently and courageously to blaze new trails through innovations. Their efforts paid off with difficulties being conquered and "two missiles and one satellite" were developed. China successfully exploded its first atom bomb on October 16,

On September 25, 2008, China successfully launched the Shenzhou VII with three astronauts on board.

1964; the first surface-to-surface missile equipped with an atomic warhead on October 27, 1966; and the first man-made satellite on April 24, 1970.

Inspired by the spirit of "two missiles and one satellite" achievement, China has made great progress in nuclear industry, aviation industry, shipbuilding industry, weaponry industry, and military and electronic industry.

In the aviation industry, China has made breakthroughs in space technology, space application, and space science. In particular, between October 15 and 16 of 2003, China successfully conducted its first manned space flight.

Yang Liwei, China's first astronaut, traveled around the earth in the spacecraft for 21 hours and 23 minutes. The century-old dream of flying into space was realized, making China the third country to independently conduct manned spaceflight. China has placed itself among the world's most advanced countries in some important fields of space technology. On October 12, 2005, China successfully launched the Shenzhou VI, which traveled around the earth 108 times, lasting 6 days and 18 hours. On October 24, 2007, the Chang'e-1 satellite was sent to space, marking the country's first success in lunar exploration. The success of Chang'e-1 was another milestone in the Chinese aviation industry, following the launch of the manmade satellite and achievement of manned spaceflight. China has realized its century-old dream of flying to the moon. This began a new era of exploring the space and its mysteries. China successfully launched the Shenzhou VII spacecraft on September 25, 2008. At about 4:50 pm Beijing time on September 27, 2008, astronaut Zhai Zhigang successfully walked out of the capsule wearing a spacesuit developed by China. It was the first extra-vehicular activity for China, and also a major leap in the country's space technology development. The vigorous development of China's aviation industry demonstrates the enhancement of its national strength and defense capability.

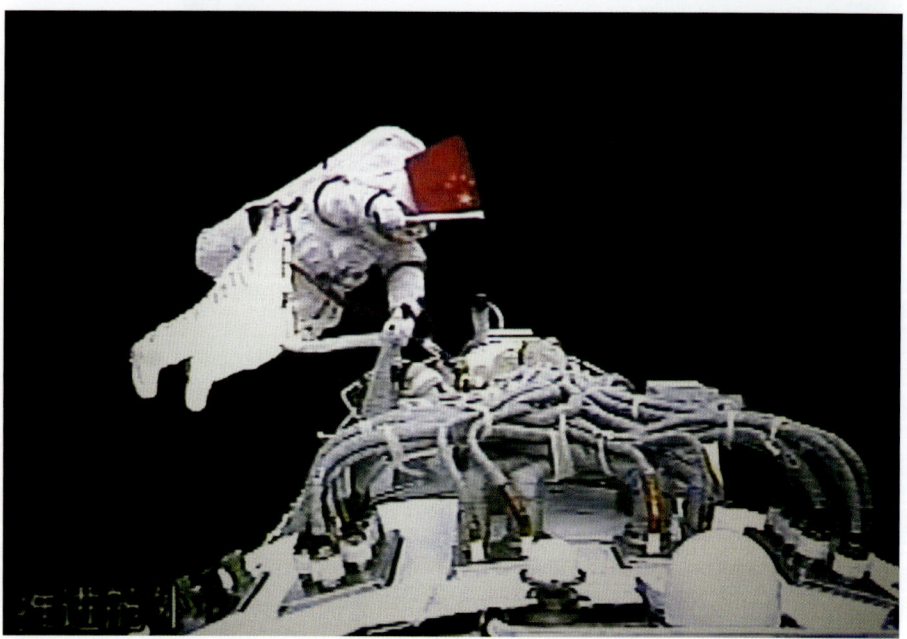

Around 16:50 on September 27, 2008, Beijing Time, Zhai Zhigang stepped out of the aircraft holding the national flag, marking the first space walk by the Chinese people.

In the space technology field, China has made great progress in research and development of civilian airplanes, such as feeder airplanes, general aircraft, and helicopters. In 2006, the multi-purpose, third-generation, advanced J-10 with independent intellectual property rights was developed by China independently, greatly enhancing the air war capacity of the Chinese air forces. Such advanced weaponry gives China the capability to oppose current foreign countries equipped with advanced fighters. A historical leap forward from the second generation to the third generation has come true.

The domestic feeder airplane "Xinzhou-60" is almost at par with foreign airplanes of the same kind in terms of safety, reliability, comfort, and maintenance, while its price is only two-third of these planes. Xinzhou-60 is another milestone of the "going out" policy for high-tech electromechanical products, marking Chinese civil aircrafts' debut into international competition.

China has made breakthroughs in nuclear power and application of nuclear technologies. The Phase II project of Qinshan Nuclear Power Station is China's first commercial nuclear power station featuring independent design, construction, management, and operation. It also boasts major breakthroughs in many technologies. For example, the control rod drive mechanism can meet the international level of 8,500,000 steps. Its comprehensive

The J-10 exhibited at the seventh China International Aviation & Aerospace Exhibition on October 28, 2008.

technologies can meet the standards of international nuclear power stations of the same kind. The Phase II project was built in keeping with international standards and its construction achieved a one-stop success without undergoing the prototype reactor stage. To sum up, the successful Phase II project demonstrates a great leap forward for China to build a small prototype reactor nuclear power station into a large commercial one and has laid the foundation for China to independently design and build million-kilowatt nuclear power stations.

In the field of shipbuilding technology, China is now capable of developing large container ships, VLCC super oil tankers, and LNG liquefied natural gas ships. The capacity and core competitive power of highly value-added ships have been enhanced. China is now stepping forward to its aim of becoming the world's No. 1 shipbuilding power.

In the field of electronic technology, China is now able to develop electronic systems, platform electronic systems, and basic electronic technology independently. Computers with the computing speed of one trillion bytes per second and various ruggedized computers have met or nearly met the international advanced level. China has edged itself among the most advanced countries in key tracking and command technologies with regard to its Telemetry Tracking and Command (TT&C) network.

New-type conventional submarine.

A Structure Uniting the Army with the People

It is essential that the army and the people stand united in the quest toward development of modern defense-related science and technology. The national defense industry can shy from its responsibilities of developing and applying new technologies and must provide materialized technology support for unification of the army with the people. The defense-related science and technology production, at the same time, follows the general economic principle, which in return, defines the industry's civil characteristic.

Since 1978, the Chinese government has always stressed the peaceful use of military industrial technology and put forward the principle of "combining the armed forces with the people, combining peacetime with wartime, giving priority to the armed forces and developing the army with the support of the people." Efforts have been made to develop dual-purpose technologies and new- and high-tech industries. Years of hard work have paid off. The Chinese defense-related science and technology industry has developed 10 sub-industries of mines, metallurgy, mechanism, electronic, light industry, chemical industry, electric power, construction material, aviation industry, and aerospace industry. In total, tens of thousands of civil products in 40 categories recorded an industrial output accounting for more than 80% of the industry's total.

The Nuclear Industrial System

The nuclear industrial system has come a long way from being based solely on the armed forces to that based on serving civil purposes over the past 50 years since the establishment of the Chinese nuclear industry. With respect to unification of the army with the people, the nuclear industry has adjusted its industrial structure and product structure, reduced military science and technology production, expanded application of the peaceful use of nuclear technologies and developed foreign technological cooperation and economic trade, paving a new road for further development of the nuclear industry. A complete industrial system with regard to nuclear power, nuclear fuel cycle, nuclear technology research and development system and nuclear equipment manufacturing system has been established. Over the past 50 years, the Chinese nuclear industry has successfully developed the atom bomb, hydrogen bomb, and nuclear submarine, making great contributions to enhancement of the national strength and the rise in its international stature.

China has made comparatively great progress in the peaceful use of nuclear power. Currently, China is home to five completed nuclear power stations: the Zhejiang Qinshan Nuclear Power Station (Phase I, II, and III),

Guangdong Daya Bay Nuclear Power Station, Lingao Nuclear Power Station, Jiangsu Tianwan Nuclear Power Station, and Shandong Haiyang Nuclear Power Station. The nuclear industry directly serves China's economic construction, and nuclear power has become the pillar product in the transfer of nuclear industry to civilian use. Until recently, 11 nuclear power units with a total installed capacity of more than 9 million kilowatts are under operation or construction, accounting for more than 2% of the country's total power supply.

The Aerospace Industry System

The aerospace industry system, founded in 1956, currently comprises two very large enterprises, China Aerospace Science and Technology Corporation and China Aerospace Science and Industry Corporation. It shoulders the responsibilities of technological production of the aerospace industry. The Chinese aerospace industry has established a complete system integrating research and development, design, production, and experiment over the past decades. Various satellite application systems and space scientific research systems, and a complete product structure covering missiles, carrier rockets, spacecraft, satellite, and satellite application system have been established. In addition, China's civil aerospace technologies have achieved a great deal in application satellite, carrier rocket, and manned spaceflight fields. The Long March series carrier rockets witnessed a success rate of 92%, with more than 80 launches.

China is now capable of developing various kinds of satellites. Technologies with regard to satellite recovery, orbit control, altitude control, and synchronous fixed point have met the international advanced standard. China has become the third country to master the technology of satellite recovery and the fifth country to independently develop and launch geostationary orbit communication satellites in the world. From April 24, 1970—when Dongfanghong-1, the country's first man-made satellite, flew into space—to May 27, 2008—when FY-3 was launched—more than 70 domestic satellites and six spacecrafts have been successfully launched from Jiuquan, Xichang, and Taiyuan. China also successfully launched more than 30 foreign satellites, reserving a place for itself in the international commercial satellite launched service market.

The Aviation Industry System

The aviation industry system, currently comprising two very large enterprises—China Aviation Industry Corporation I and China Aviation Industry Corporation II—undertakes the responsibilities of scientific production. A comparatively complete system covering aviation scientific research,

The ARJ21 feeder line airplane with fully independent intellectual property rights was released by the end of 2007.

experiment, and manufacturing has been established through decades of research and development. Enterprises concentrating on special design and research and manufacturing of aircrafts, aeroengines, airborne equipment, and airborne weapons have been set up. Research and experiment institutions on aerodynamic force, intension, auto-control, pilot flying, materials, techniques, and computing technologies have also been well established. The product structure with regard to military and civil aircraft, helicopters, aeroengines, and airborne equipment and weapons is complete. As for the civil aircraft industry, it recorded achievements in the development of general aircraft and new feeder aircraft. The Chinese civil aircraft industry started with modeling aircrafts based on foreign light aircrafts. Fifty years of hard work has paid rich dividends. Eight series including more than 30 types of passenger and cargo aircraft, general aircraft, and civil helicopters have come into production. More than 1,400 units have been produced.

As for international cooperation, cooperation with regard to production, joint research, feasibility research, and pre-stage argumentation with McDonnell Douglas, Eurocopter, Singapore Technologies Engineering Ltd (ST), and ST German and European Airbus Corporation are also vigorous besides subcontracting the manufacture of components of foreign aircrafts and engines.

In February 2007, the State Council approved a plan to develop large aircrafts in Shanghai. In May 2008, Commercial Aircraft Corporation of China, Ltd, was officially set up, marking the advent of China's large aircraft manufacturing industry.

The Shipbuilding Industry System

The shipbuilding industry system, comprising China State Shipbuilding Corporation and China Shipbuilding Industry Corporation, are the two main enterprises under the Chinese shipbuilding industry that have undertaken the task of scientific production. Through years of development, the industry has played a more important role in economic development and has become a manufacturing department of major technical equipment. A powerful experienced scientific research team with high-level scientific research ability and a large-scale manufacturing team have been established for manufacturing modern marine forces equipment, such as nuclear submarines, missile destroyers, oceangoing space instrumentation ships, civil ships, and marine engineering equipment with high-performance and high added value. The shipbuilding industry for civil use has already become a highly competitive pillar export industry among China's electromechanical industries. In recent years, China's shipbuilding output has continuously increased, ranking it third in the world for 13 consecutive years. In 2007, the Chinese shipbuilding industry recorded a production of 18 million tons, an increase of 25% as compared with 2006 and contracted new orders of 70 million tons. Currently, more than 80% of the ships produced by China will be exported to 128 countries and regions. The general long- and medium-term goal of the Chinese shipbuilding industry is to establish an industrial base that can compete with those of the foreign shipbuilding industries, and to develop an industrial pattern centering on large-scale corporations and combining scale and specialization. Overall progress in industrial technology, supporting facilities, and labor productivity has been achieved and has met the international advanced level.

The Chinese electronic military industry has set up a pattern with a complete range of systems including electronic military scientific research and production. After 20 years of reform and development, China now is capable of developing an independent electronic system and basic electronic technologies. In China, electronic military enterprises can manufacture thousands of electronic components and related equipment and materials. These enterprises are also capable of manufacturing radars, investigation systems, comprehensive electronic warfare systems, navigation systems, communication equipment,

An anti-riot robot exhibited at the high-tech achievements exchange fair.

large-, medium- and small-sized military computers, servers, working stations, and rugged and embedded computers. Integration of large systems can also be realized. The complete product structure has also been formed.

The Weapons Industrial System

Currently, China North Industries Group Corporation and China South Industries Group Corporation shoulder the responsibilities of scientific production. Some local military industrial enterprises also shoulder part of the responsibilities of scientific production. The Chinese weapons industry has, after decades of development, moved from production of traditional weapons to that of high-tech weapons; uncontrolled attack to precise attack; and operations with single type weapons from ones featuring system opposition to weapon system opposition. An independent and complete scientific research and production system has been set up that meets the international advanced standards. As for the development of military products, the Chinese weapons industry can manufacture tanks, armored vehicles, guns, ammunition, guided weapons, small arms, powders, dynamites and so on. The production of civil products covers mechanical, chemical, and opto-electronic fields. The industry, to some extent, is qualified to develop some major industries, such as engineering mechanical, power transmission, and engineering blasting.

Today, the system of uniting the armed forces with the people involves more than just the transformation of military technologies for civilian use. Privately owned high-tech enterprises have been developing rapidly. They boast stronger technological innovations and scientific development ability; some technologies are above military levels. Making full use of the privately owned technology enterprises and encouraging them to dedicate themselves to research and development of military production is a problem that needs to be solved. In order to do so, the Chinese defense-related industry has earnestly adhered to uniting the armed forces with the people and integrating the military resources with civilian ones. China should increase inter-promotion and coordinated development between defense-related technologies and privately owned ones. On the one hand, efforts should be made to make full use of military resources in order to push forward the development of the national economy; on the other hand, military monopoly should be broken. In particular, more privately owned high-tech enterprises should participate in the construction of national defense and speed up the development of weapons.

The China International Defence Electronics Exhibition 2008. A training missile of the domestic WF170 Tomahawk cruise missiles attract visitors.

The new main battle tanks.

Reform and Development of the Defense-related Science and Technology Industry

China's defense-related science and technology industry has been expanding its reform based on previous achievements. Adjustments and optimization of industrial structure go on smoothly, and the mechanism of uniting the armed forces with the people has been improved. Gradual transformation in managing the model and upgrading the industry has been achieved so as to enhance product quality and production efficiency.

Adjustments of the Defense-related Science and Technology Industry

In line with the general plan of "small core, large coordination, and uniting the armed forces with the people," military scientific research and manufacturing capacities must be further improved; continuous adjustments should be conducted on product and industrial structures; specialized production should be promoted; and the integration of domestic and foreign markets and military and civilian resources should not be neglected. China should lay more stress on the international cooperation of scientific research and development of military products, further expanding military product markets, adhering to information-based and industrialized development pattern; and improve manufacturing level, and research and development level in particular.

By making full use of market mechanisms, China has expedited the grouping of the industry and structural adjustments. A new organizing model has also been set up in line with the development of the industry.

The industry should commit itself to strengthening the dual-purpose research and development capacity and adjusting the military-industrial technology structure. By arming military-industrial production with digital technology, the research and development and manufacturing capacities of weapons equipment have been much enhanced. In addition, the core capacities including designing, general assembly testing, and system integration have been enhanced through the optimization of scientific research and development structure. Besides, China has better levered the technology introduction and independent research and development. On the one hand, the country spares no efforts to introduce foreign technologies; on the other hand, it pays attention to innovations of microelectronic, optoelectronic, and new material fields. By concentrating its strength on supporting large-size aircrafts, civil satellites, and large-scale nuclear stations, China has made a leap forward. A series of adjustments and reforms of the industry have made contributions to the Development of the Western Region, and have helped revive the old industry bases in North China and have helped in the construction of Tianjin Binhai New Area. In short, the development of the military-industrial production must be in line with economic development.

Improvement of the Management Mechanism

China has set up a new defense-related industrial mechanism that is in line with the socialist market economy system and development of weapon equipment.

China has begun to reform the current defense-related science and technology management system. In line with the principle of "economic regulation, market oversight, social governance, and public service," emphasis will be placed on service, guiding, and supervising work. Relationship among the government, military-industrial corporations, and enterprises has been well balanced. Regulations and laws have been improved to regulate management and enhance management efficiency. To meet the requirements of association management, the optimization of the management structure has already been placed on the agenda, and functions in terms of communication, service, and supervision have also been improved.

China has been improving the current operating mechanism of the industry. Efforts have been made to set up and improve the "four mechanisms," namely, competitive mechanism, evaluation mechanism, supervision mechanism, and encouragement mechanism, keeping competitive mechanism as the core and breaking the state military supplies order system, placing key emphasis on the driving forces of development. Technological achievements serve both military and civilian purposes, and military-civilian communication is finally being realized. Problems that hinder the development of HR must be solved through HR development and management mechanisms.

Reforms of Defense-related Science and Technology Institutes and Manufacturing Enterprises

Enterprises, scientific research institutes, and universities should utilize their advantageous situation to set up a scientific research and development union or industrial technology innovation union, through which profits, losses, and risks are shared. Integration of production, teaching, and research will be the key for the establishment of the innovation system. Market-oriented reform of scientific research institutes should be pushed forward alongside the optimization of scientific layout and resource allocation to better lever economic development and national defense building. China has long been placing prime emphasis on technological assembly through balancing defense-related scientific research and enterprise manufacturing, with a defense-related science and industry management pattern taking shape. Relevant departments must better deal with problems on patents and compensation of values of defense-related scientific achievements.

A modern military industrial enterprise system has been set up based on the success of the reform of state-owned enterprises. Starting with the reform of property rights system, construction of modern enterprise system has been sped up, transformation of enterprises to joint-stock ones have already been launched and corporate governance has been improved. The government should encourage people to take part in scientific research and development of military-industrial products and set up an access and withdrawal system for domestic and foreign military product manufacturing bodies. In this way, the military-civilian interaction and coordinated system will be formed gradually. It is necessary to deepen the military-industrial investment mechanism, encourage diversified investment, and establish a new investment mechanism. In June 2006, a privately owned enterprise in Shaanxi signed a contract to manufacture weapons for the United Nations Peacekeeping Force, the first privately owned enterprise involved in weapons equipment manufacturing. Besides, more than 100 non-public sectors have become equipment suppliers for land-based armed forces in recent years.

The long-distance attack exercise of the bomber.

Management of Military Product Export and Peaceful use of Military-Industrial Technology

China not only helps other foreign countries in national defense construction but also supports them in peaceful use of military-industrial technologies.

China firmly adheres to the following principles regarding military product exports:

(1) The export of such products should help the recipient nation increase its defense capacity appropriately;
(2) It must not impair peace, security, and stability of the relevant region and the world as a whole; and
(3) It must not be used to interfere in the recipient state's internal affairs.

China persistently supports activities involving the peaceful utilization of nuclear technology. Pakistan's first nuclear station jointly set up by the country and China has been put into operation, and the second one is under construction. The nuclear power generated has made contributions to Pakistan's economic development.

China has always opposed the proliferation of weapons of mass destruction (WMD) and their means of delivery. As a member state of the *Non-Proliferation*

FYI
FOR YOUR INFORMATION

CHINA JOINS IN THE SYSTEMS OF ARMS CONTROL, DISARMAMENT, AND NON-PROLIFERATION

Nuclear

Additional Protocol II to the *Treaty on Prohibition of Nuclear Weapons in Latin America and the Caribbean*

Additional Protocol II and III to the *South Pacific Nuclear Free Zone Treaty*

Treaty by the People's Republic of China and the International Atomic Energy Agency on the Safeguards in China

Convention on the Physical Protection of Nuclear Material

Treaty on the Prohibition of the Embedment of Nuclear Weapons and Other WMDs on the Seabed and the Ocean Floor

Treaty on the Non-Proliferation of Nuclear Weapons

Additional Protocol I and II to the African Nuclear-Weapon-Free Zone

Comprehensive Nuclear Test Ban Treaty

Additional Protocol to the Treaty by the People's Republic of China and the International Atomic Energy Agency on the Safeguards in China

Chemical

Convention on the Prohibition of the Development, Production, Stockpiling, and Use of Chemical Weapons and on Their Destruction

Biological

Protocol for the Prohibition of the Use in War of Asphyxiating, Poisonous, or Other Gases

Convention on the Prohibition of the Development, Production, and Stockpiling of Bacteriological (Biological) and Toxin Weapons and on Their Destruction

Conventional

Convention on Prohibition or Restriction on the Use of Certain Conventional Weapons That May Be Deemed to Be Excessively Injurious or to Have Indiscriminate Effects and the Additional Protocol I, II, and III

Others

Antarctic Treaty

Treaty on Principles Governing the Activities of States in the Exploration and Use of Outer Space, Including the Moon and Other Celestial Bodies

Convention on Registration of Objects Launched into Outer Space

Convention on the Prohibition of Military or Any Other Hostile Use of Environmental Modification Techniques

of Nuclear Weapons (NPT) CWC and BWC, China has strictly adhered to the principles, abided by its obligations, and supported non-proliferation activities.

All along, the Chinese government has adopted a very prudent and responsible attitude toward control of non-proliferation export and has strictly controlled the export of sensitive materials and technologies related to proliferation of WMD and their carriers. It has improved the control mechanism and set up a law-governed system on export control.

The Chinese government has issued a series of laws and regulations, such as the *Regulations on Nuclear Export Control and Regulations on the Control of Nuclear Dual-Use Items and Related Technologies Export,* since 1997, covering a wider range of areas. Therefore, a compete export control system has been formed.

The Chinese government believes that the proliferation of WMD and their means of delivery have complicated roots. Anti-proliferation activities should adopt both temporary and permanent solutions through a series of political and diplomatic means. Establishing a fair and rational new international order and realizing the universal improvement in international relations are the fundamental ways to eliminate the threat of the WMD and the premise for sound development of the international anti-proliferation course. Establishment of a fair, rational, and effective international nonproliferation regime is the final purpose of the international community. The international community should, on the basis of principles such as undiminished security for all countries, guarantee that each country is equal in making use of advanced technologies. Strengthening the current nonproliferation regime or establishing a new one should, on the basis of universal participation and democratic decision-making, give full play to the United Nations.

The Chinese government is willing—together with the international community—to contribute to the promotion and development of the non-proliferation regime, and peace, stability, and development of the world.

Chapter 8

....

Safeguarding World Peace and Promoting Common Development

Historical evidence indicates that only by opening up to the outside world can an armed force become stronger. A modern armed force should keep pace with the times. China is making great efforts to place itself among the other nations in the international community. The Chinese government is committed to safeguarding world peace and promoting common development. China insists on dealing with its foreign military relations independently and on engaging in military exchanges and cooperation based on the Five Principles of Peaceful Coexistence. The Chinese armed forces have created an image for themselves— a mighty and civilized force and a force of peace. The Chinese armed forces have been in touch with the international community since the 21st century. They are now playing an ever larger role in international affairs and have become an important force in safeguarding world peace and promoting common development.

Foreign Military Contact

Military diplomacy should serve the state's overall diplomacy and the modernization of national defense and the armed forces. With this purpose in mind, the PLA has actively engaged in external contacts and exchanges in a flexible and practical manner, and made sustained efforts for enhanced mutual trust, friendship, and cooperation with armed forces of other countries, and for regional and world peace, stability, and development. These military diplomatic activities include exchange of high-level military visits, international bilateral and multilateral negotiations, exhibition of weapon equipment, international military and trade negotiations, international military and academic exchanges, international cooperation of military technologies, international military, and cultural exchanges, and international military sports activities.

To date, China has established military relations with more than 150 countries and 107 military attaché offices in Chinese embassies abroad. Meanwhile, 85 countries have set up military attaché offices in China. The open, pragmatic, and active military contacts with foreign countries have introduced the peace-loving Chinese armed forces to the international community and bridged communication gaps with foreign armed forces for further cooperation and common development.

In recent years, China has increased its contact with many foreign military delegations. In 2007, the United States Secretary of Defense and Chairman of the Joint Chiefs of Staff visited China; the minister of the Ministry of National Defense visited Russia, promoting the development of China-Russia strategic partnership of coordination; and the minister of the Ministry of National

Minister Liang Guanglie of the Ministry of Defense visiting Volgograd, Russia, April 27, 2009.

The Aerobatic Demonstration Team of the Chinese Air Force.

Defense visited Japan. Also, there were exchanges between the military officials of China and European Union countries. In recent years, China has improved its military relations with its neighboring countries. And, the Chinese armed forces have also maintained close ties with armed forces in Africa and Latin America.

As China's reform and opening up speeds up and the construction of the marine forces develops, exchange visits between the Chinese and foreign marine forces have increased, contributing greatly to the promotion of friendship.

Demonstration flights by the armed air forces is another way to develop foreign military contacts. The demonstration flight team of the PLA, "8·1 Demonstration Flight Team," serves as the guard of honor in the air. The team has contributed greatly in demonstrating the martial bearing of the PLA and has never met with any accidents.

The Chinese armed forces actively participate in various military academic conferences that are significant for knowledge about the academic trends and military achievement exchanges, and attracting foreign technologies and professionals. China's non-governmental military bodies are also actively participating in foreign activities. For example, the China

International Strategies Association, a national non-governmental academic association on international strategies, has regular contact with foreign institutes on strategies and international issues. A series of activities, such as visit exchanges and bilateral or multilateral seminars have helped to promote mutual understanding and friendship.

Various art troupes of the PLA often visit many foreign countries and regions. At the same time, China has welcomed various foreign visiting art troupes. Cultural communication and friendship have been improved through theses exchanges. The PLA is also home to sports troupes, which participate in international sports competitions. In February 1979, the PLA Physical Culture and Sports Committee officially joined the International Military Sports Council (CISM) and began to participate in various conferences and competitions held by the CISM, and the Chinese sports persons have achieved good results.

As an important component of China's overall diplomatic ties, China's foreign military contacts make strengthening friendly cooperation and the promotion of peaceful development their goals. The Chinese government—in promoting the multi-directional, multi-level, and all-round cooperation with Russia—pays attention to cooperation on key defense problems. Senior officials of China and Russia pay regular visits to each country, and

The military band of the PLA takes part in the 2004 Edinburgh Military Music Festival.

The Chinese ambassador and military attaché to the United States speak with Chinese and American commanders. On September 7, 2006, Chinese naval vessels visit Pearl Harbor in Hawaii for four days.

the ministers of Chinese and Russian Ministry of National Defense have also met several times. Therefore, the China-Russia strategic partnership of coordination has been strengthened, guaranteeing global strategic balance. On March 14, 2008, the first direct line connecting the Ministry of National Defense of the PRC and the Russia Federal National Defense became active, and the ministers of the two countries talked through the line for the first time.

China and the United States share the same interests and shoulder the same responsibilities for world peace and common development. However, development of the China-US relationship has not been very smooth, as is evident by the intermittent visits between senior officials of the two countries. In recent years, visits between the two countries' military delegations have increased, playing an active role in the world's safety and stability. On April 10, 2008, the direct line connecting the Ministry of National Defense of the PRC and the US Department of Defense became active enabling the exchange of opinions on common issues between the ministers on both sides.

Military relationship between China and the Southeast Asian and South Asian countries has also developed well.

Chinese military officials also visited part of the European and third-world countries, strengthening military cooperation and promoting the development of a multi-polar world.

The multilateral cooperation between China and the Central Asian countries and Russia has also strengthened considerably, playing an important role in safeguarding regional stability and safety. In April 1996, the heads of state of China, Russia, Kazakhstan, Kyrgyzstan, and Tajikistan met in Shanghai for the first time and signed the *Agreement on Confidence-Building in the Military Field along the Border Areas.* On June 14, 2001, Uzbekistan joined in the agreement; hence, the establishment of Shanghai Cooperation Organization (SCO). The SCO propagates the "Shanghai Spirit" that features mutual trust, mutual benefit, equality, consultation, respect for diverse civilizations, and seeking common development. A common consensus has been reached that the members would promote military cooperation, fight against international terrorism, ethnic separatism, and religious extremism. This is especially helpful for world peace and common development in the 21st century.

China's military contact with foreign countries focuses on five points:

First, friendly cooperation not only involves the developing countries but also developed ones. The foreign affairs department will also strengthen cooperation with military attaché offices.

Second, the Chinese government will further develop foreign military economic cooperation with foreign countries. China has actively and prudently carried out military trade on the basis of mutual equality and benefit since the reform and opening up, providing more opportunities for the Chinese defense-related science and technology industry.

Third, military contacts must be in line with the creation of a favorable international environment. China has been sparing no effort in building a well-off society in a wholesome manner, which must be accomplished under a peaceful international environment. The military contacts should, through various activities, strengthen military co-operation and communication, maintain regional peace and stability, ease external pressures, and help China gain more initiative.

Fourth, military contacts should serve defense-related modernization. Centering on the defense-related modernization and keeping pace with the trends, China should learn from other countries and make full use of the international division of labor and exchanges of military products to introduce advanced technologies and equipment and conduct military and academic communications.

Lastly, China will let the world know about its independent foreign policy of peace. China has always been a staunch supporter of safeguarding world peace and promoting common development through various military activities.

Chinese soldiers perform martial arts at the first China-Tajikistan joint anti-terrorism exercise conducted within the border of Tajikistan.

Chinese Armed Forces Actively Take Part in UN Peacekeeping Operations

In accordance with the decisions of the UN Security Council and General Assembly of the UN, the UN peacekeeping operation dispatches military forces to conflict areas with the purpose of preventing local conflicts from escalating or re-occurring. As a permanent member of the UN Security Council, China has always valued and supported the UN in its efforts to play a positive role in safeguarding international peace and security under the guidance of the purpose and principles of the UN Charter.

Since April 1990 when China first dispatched five military observers, it has sent a total of 14,650 personnel members to participate in 18 peacekeeping operations of the United Nations around the world by the end of October 2009. Thus, China became a UN Security Council permanent member that sends the largest number of troops in UN-led peacekeeping missions. Currently, there are 1,861 Chinese peacekeeping officers and soldiers in five UN peacekeeping task areas, engaged in engineering, medical, and transportation missions. Among these personnel, eight commanders and soldiers have died while on duty, and many people were injured.

On March 25, 2008, 335 commanders and soldiers and 8 staff officers and military observers were awarded with the Medal of Honor by the UN for their contribution to the peacekeeping activities.

China, in adherence with the UN Charter, continues to take part in peacekeeping operations. In February 2001, China officially joined the Grade I Stand-By mechanism of the UN peacekeeping operation. China is ready to provide engineering, medical care, and transportation support services.

For example, Chinese military personnel went to Congo in April 2003; the first 60 military staff members went to Libya in December 2003; on October 17, 2004, 90 Chinese peacekeeping members went to Haiti—the first time that China sent its military personnel to a country that did not have diplomatic relations with China. On August 27, 2007, a Chinese military commander was nominated as a senior commander of the UN peacekeeping force by the Secretary-General of the UN. This demonstrates that China's efforts in the peacekeeping operations have been affirmed by the international community. On November 23, 2007, the first batch of Chinese military personnel went to Darfur of Sudan—the first peacekeeping force dispatched by the UN in Darfur. It was expected that China would send a total of more than 300 commanders and soldiers to Darfur.

Chinese peacekeeping troops have won great acclaim from the leading bodies of UN peacekeeping missions and local residents for their excellent style and ability to fulfill the tasks with great efficiency. In 2008, the piracy problem became greatly prominent in the Gulf of Aden and Somali waters, seriously affecting the security of shipping vessels and personnel of various countries in the world including China, and forming a great threat to the ships delivering humanitarian supplies by international institutions to Somalia; the pirates became an international menace. The UN Security Council passed numerous resolutions authorizing various countries to take action in accordance with the UN Charter and combat piracy in the Somali waters. The Somalian government also called on other countries to enter its territorial waters to combat piracy. The Chinese government decided to send two destroyers and a supply ship from the South Sea Fleet of PLA Navy to embark on a journey on December 26, 2008 to the above-mentioned area in order to escort ships requiring assistance. This is a concrete embodiment of China actively fulfilling its international obligations, displaying the image of a big responsible country, and safeguarding world stability and peace, especially peace and security in the Gulf of Aden and Somalian waters.

These successful missions also demonstrated the confidence and ability of the Chinese military in responding to a variety of security threats and accomplishing diversified military tasks.

In view of the frequent pirate attacks, China believes that the international community should further strengthen maritime escort operations while the participating countries should improve the coordination of escort operations in order to prevent the occurrence of pirate attacks more effectively. In line with the requirement of the Working Group 1 of the Contact Group on Piracy off the coast of Somalia, China invited relevant countries and organizations participating in the fight against Somali pirates to attend the Gulf of Aden Escort Coordination Conference between November 6 and 7, 2009 in Beijing, and further explored ways to introduce division escort cooperation in the Gulf of Aden. China holds a positive and open attitude toward escort international cooperation, and is willing to carry out various forms of bilateral and multilateral escort cooperation with all relevant countries and organizations under the framework of international law and relevant resolutions of the UN Security Council so as to jointly cope with the threat of piracy in Somalia.

The Chinese Navy escorting warships in the Gulf of Aden on January 6, 2009.

International Anti-terrorist Cooperation and Joint Military Exercises

The world is not a peaceful place yet; unilateralism still exists. Terrorism is rampant. At the same time, most of the problems the world faces today are of such complexity that they cannot be addressed by any single nation acting alone.

Terrorism hampers world peace, and today, the issue is more serious than ever. Growing terrorism has caused great turbulence in the world.

China actively participates in anti-terrorist activities. From August 6 to 12, 2003, China and other member states of the SCO jointly held an anti-terrorist exercise called "Joint-2003." The SCO Anti-Terrorism Organization commenced operations after June 2004. From August 9 to 17, 2007, a joint anti-terrorism exercise, "A Mission of Peace – 2007," was held in Urumchi of Sinkiang and Čeľabinsk of Russia, and five member states of the SCO participated in the same. The exercise in Čeľabinsk was the first transnational military dispatch conducted by China.

After the "9/11 attacks," the Chinese and American intelligence agencies began to cooperate, and Consultation Mechanism to Strengthen Military Maritime Safety was re-established. On October 24, 2003, the minister of the Ministry of National Defense of the PRC was invited by the minister of the US Department of Defense. The two ministers conducted a friendly discussion on international and regional safety and the relationship between the two countries. In September and November of 2006, China and the United States conducted joint exercises at sea near the western coast of the United States and South China Sea, respectively. In November 2007, the newly appointed

The Sino-Russian troops for "Peace Mission 2009" launch a joint anti-terrorism exercise at the Taonan tactical training base, Northeast China, Jilin Province, July 23, 2009.

The PLA navy parade at the Yellow Sea off Qingdao to celebrate its 60th anniversary on April 23, 2009.

minister of the US Department of Defense visited China, further strengthening the military cooperation between the two countries.

China has started participating in bilateral and multilateral joint military exercises in keeping with various demands since 2002 to enhance cooperation and communication with some important countries. In recent years, China has, together with some member states of the SCO, conducted several joint military exercises, covering a wider area, such as anti-terrorism and anti-smuggling.

On October 22, 2003, the search and rescue exercise, "Dolphin 0310," was jointly held in the East China Sea by the Chinese and the visiting Pakistani warships. This was the Chinese marine forces' first joint exercise in the non-traditional fields of security. On August 6, 2004, the Chinese and Pakistani armed forces conducted a joint anti-terrorism military exercise—Friendship 2004—at the China-Pakistan Border. This was the first joint military exercise between China and Pakistan. On November 25, 2005, a visiting fleet composed of a missile destroyer and a comprehensive depot ship, together with Pakistani marine forces, conducted a joint search and rescue exercise in the non-traditional field of security in the northern Arabian Sea. From December

US Marine Corps Commandant Gen. James Conway visits the amphibious landing training ground of the South Sea Fleet and observes the anti-terrorism exercise on April 3, 2008.

11 to 18 of 2006, China and Pakistan conducted a joint anti-terrorism exercise—"Friendship 2006"—in Abbottabad, Pakistan.

On November 14, 2003, the Chinese marine warship and the visiting Indian marine warship performed a joint search and rescue exercise, "Dolphin 0311," in China East Sea near Shanghai. This was the first joint exercise conducted by China and India in the non-traditional field of security. On December 1, 2005, a fleet composed of a Chinese missile destroyer and a comprehensive depot ship, together with an Indian warship, conducted a joint search and rescue exercise—"China-India Friend 2005"—in the Northern Indian Ocean. In 2007, China and India conducted a joint military exercise named "Hand in Hand 2007."

On March 16, 2004, the Chinese and French marine forces performed a joint military exercise off the sea near Qingdao. In this exercise, the French helicopter successfully landed on the Chinese warship, as did the Chinese helicopter.

On June 20, 2004, a joint search and rescue exercise was successfully held by the Chinese and English marine forces at the Yellow Sea near Qingdao. It was the first time that China and England conducted a joint exercise, and

15 foreign naval attachés in China were invited to watch and learn from the exercise.

On August 18, 2005, the significant joint military exercise, "A Mission of Peace 2005" conducted by China and Russia first started in Russia and then in Shandong, further strengthening the cooperation between the two countries. From May 11 to 23, 2007, the Chinese "Xiangfan" missile frigate participated in the "International Maritime Defense Exhibition Asia (IMDEX Asia) 2007" and "The 2nd Western Naval Forum and Multilateral Offshore Exercise" in Singapore. In all, 15 warships from 12 countries took part in the exercise. Peacefulness and good neighborliness have long been prized by the Chinese people. The new security concept proposed by China seeks to pursue common development based on mutual benefit and cooperation.

The More Open Chinese Armed Forces

Firmly adhering to the principle of self defense, the Chinese armed forces endeavor to make "safeguarding peace" their goal and build themselves into more open and modernized forces. The Chinese armed forces are now integrating themselves into the international community through a wider channel.

In 1995, China first published white papers on arms control and disarmament agreements. By 2006, China had published five white papers on China's National Defense. The Ministry of National Defense established a new release system through which relevant news on quake-relief work following the Wenchuan Earthquake was released on May 18, 2008.

Since 2000, the Chinese government has invited and hosted foreign military observers and military attachés to China to watch military exercises. On September 27, 2005, military observers from 24 countries watched the live exercises in Beijing. For the first time, the Chinese PLA Second Artillery Corps was opened to foreign military commanders, demonstrating that the Chinese military has become more transparent to the outside world.

The Chinese armed forces not only actively invite foreign military forces to visit China, but also, in turn, visit foreign countries. Various delegations or military observers have been sent to foreign countries to watch military exercises as well as the Cobra Gold Military Exercises jointly held by United States and Thailand. On November 28, 2007, China's "Shenzhen" missile destroyer visited Japan; 345 commanders and soldiers were on board. It was the first time

On November 28, 2007, a Chinese missile destroyer—the first Chinese military vessel to visit Japan—casts anchor at the Harumi Harbor of the Tokyo Bay.

that the Chinese marine forces visited Japan. The Chinese armed forces can learn much about foreign advanced militaries' theories and practices through these series of visits.

In order to maintain mutual trust and an environment that strengthens communication, the Chinese armed forces actively conduct bilateral defense consultations and take part in security dialogues, guaranteeing mutual trust. The Chinese government has already established consultation mechanisms with main foreign powers to strengthen military security. Also, China has gradually conducted communication and dialogue with its neighboring countries and even distant countries to expand mutual trust channels.

On August 20, 2009, after being approved by the CMC, the website of the Ministry of National Defense of the People's Republic of China went live. With the domain www.mod.gov.cn, the website now has two versions in Chinese and English. The website has drawn widespread concern from viewers at home and abroad, and its traffic reached 1.25 billion in the first three months since its launch. As the official website of the Ministry of National Defense of the People's Republic of China, it mainly releases authoritative information on China's national defense and military building. The website of the Ministry of National

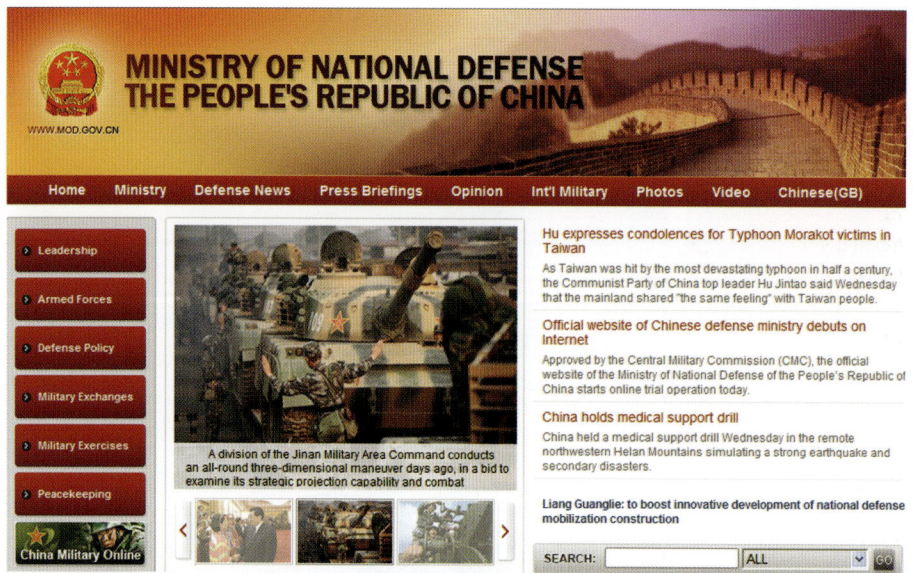

A screenshot of the website of the Ministry of National Defense of the People's Republic of China when it started its trial operation on August 20, 2009.

Defense is aimed at transmitting voices of the Chinese military, publicizing China's national defense policies, strengthening exchanges and cooperation with foreign militaries, showcasing the good image as a mighty and civilized army of peace, and promoting the modernization and building of China's national defense and military. The move will undoubtedly greatly enhance the transparency of China's military and China's national defense.

INDEX